Praise for

The Accidental Business Nomad

"In an age when the time to read books is getting fierce competition from the magnetic pull of the mobile screen, we need to know that a book we are thinking of picking up is really worth reading. This book is! Beautiful writing. Important message. Relevant topic. And did I say beautifully written? Read it."

—Fredrik Haren, global keynote speaker and
author of the bestseller *The Idea Book*

"Relatable, candid and hilariously true!"

—Ritu G. Mehrish, global speaker and
author of *Leader's Block*

"Culture shock. Immersion. Authenticity. Reconciliation. Success. Kyle's book *The Accidental Business Nomad* is not only an adventurous tale of entrepreneurship but a guide to navigating the new world where East and West come together on a daily basis."

—Dr. Parag Khanna, author of *The Future is Asian*

"This is the Indiana Jones of international business."

—Csaba Toth, author of *Uncommon Sense in
Unusual Times*

"Kyle Hegarty's new book *The Accidental Business Nomad* really resonates. Kyle is a seasoned business executive with a great sense of humor, a healthy dose of self-deprecation, and a keen instinct about how to cross cultures effectively. A fun and insightful read!"

—Andy Molinsky, Ph.D., award-winning author of
Global Dexterity and Reach

"If you wish for a beer chat with an experienced intercultural deal-maker before you take your business from West to East or vice-versa, here is your chance. Kyle's stories of global business tribulations and triumphs will give you the clarity you need."

—Gábor Holch, East-West leadership
consultant, author, and speaker

"Kyle Hegarty's new book, *The Accidental Business Nomad*, is definitely in the can't-put-it-down category. Hegarty engages the reader in some of the most complex communication issues of our global economy. He takes us from culture shock to cultural competency with colorful examples that make us laugh and cringe at the same time. Using his extensive business experience in Asia, he highlights the cross-cultural challenges involved in working globally and take us from ignorance to mastery. His entertaining style uses the power of storytelling and the expertise of academic research to engage and educate. Hegarty defuses the multiple landmines of globalization that too often remain invisible to aspiring businesses and account for their failure."

—Deborah Levine, founder and editor-in-chief of
the *American Diversity Report*

"Cultural differences, which may be charming on holiday, are far less so when your salary depends on understanding them. There is no substitute for doing your research, but in this easy to read account of his struggles, [Kyle] generously allows the reader to learn from his own mistakes—and hopefully make less of their own."

—Patti McCarthy, author of *Cultural Chemistry:
Simple Strategies for Bridging Cultural Gaps*

"A much-needed survival guide for any global leader who has left a board meeting, team call or conversation feeling like they didn't hit the mark." —Diana Wu David, author of *Future Proof*

"Wise and funny, this book is packed with sage advice and keen insights gained from the author's hard-won experience."

—Henry Laurence, associate professor of
Government at Bowdoin College

The Accidental Business Nomad

A Survival Guide for Working
Across a Shrinking Planet

Kyle D. Hegarty

NICHOLAS BREALEY
PUBLISHING

BOSTON · LONDON

To my father. The real international entrepreneur of the family

---

First published in 2020 by Nicholas Brealey Publishing
An imprint of John Murray Press

An Hachette UK company

25 24 23 22 21 20   1 2 3 4 5 6 7 8 9 10

Epigraph on page 35 taken from Liar's Poker by Michael Lewis, courtesy of
W. W. Norton & Company, Inc.
Epigraph on page 119 courtesy of Diana David Wu
Epipraph on page 183 taken from Anthony Bourdain Thinks
You're Crazy for Eating Airplane Food by Belle Cushing, published by
Bon Appétit, May 9, 2016, courtesy of Condé Nast.

A CIP catalogue record for this title is available from the British Library

Library of Congress Control Number: 2019957576

ISBN 978-1-5293-2907-0
US eBook ISBN 978-1-5293-2910-0
UK eBook ISBN 978-1-5293-2908-7

Printed and bound in the United States of America.

John Murray Press policy is to use papers that are natural, renewable, and
recyclable products and made from wood grown in sustainable forests.
The logging and manufacturing processes are expected to conform to the
environmental regulations of the country of origin.

John Murray Press Ltd
Carmelite House
50 Victoria Embankment
London EC4Y 0DZ
Tel: 020 3122 6000

Nicholas Brealey Publishing
Hachette Book Group
53 State Street
Boston, MA 02109, USA
Tel: (617) 263 1834

www.nbuspublishing.com

Contents

Acknowledgments

This adventure could not have happened without the patience and support of my wife Leah and my two young boys who had to put up with my vacant stares and many weekends hiding away writing and editing. Leah, you were the accidental editor who saved my story lines. Special thanks to my family back in the US who have always been globally minded and to my mother for making sure I took the leap to study abroad many years ago. I'm grateful to my in-laws, especially Anne who was my first unofficial editor and cheerleader.

Thanks to my agent Leah Spiro who took a risk on a crazy guy rambling about slap dragons. My editors, Alison Hankey from Nicholas Brealey who somehow understood what I was trying to say, DeeDee Slewka who helped me say it, and Iain Campbell and his team for getting some of these more colorful stories past the legal department. To my friends who endured my endless ramblings and who gave guidance and encouragement. A thank you to all of the clients and partners who wrestled alongside me as we worked through these global challenges and whose shared experiences helped form the backbone of this book. Also, thank you to all the people who went through that internship program. You all took a massive chance and it's been fantastic to watch so many of you move on to great careers, especially those of you who started your own businesses. This has been one hell of a journey and I can't wait to start the next one.

Author's Note

We use generalizations all the time to describe groups of people. "The Chinese exchange business cards with two hands," "tech companies are always doing things this way," "men always say things like that," "well, she's a millennial, so..." and so on. There's a fine line between constructive generalizing and malicious stereotyping. The problem is knowing where the line is. Here's an example.

I led a workshop in Mumbai where the organizer said the day would start at 8 am. Yeah, right. Nothing in India starts on time, certainly not 8 am. I rolled in at 8:15 to find a room packed with attendees patiently waiting for me. Ugh. I was guilty of taking a generalization about the lack of timeliness in India and converting it into a stereotype. I didn't mean to, but I did.

This book is about what it's like doing business across the globe and across cultures. One of the big conclusions I draw is that data-driven generalizations about different working styles can help people understand and adjust to different work situations. There is data that shows that India is more time-flexible than the US. We can probably agree on this. But it doesn't mean you should show up late.

This is tricky, and I dig into these broad generalizations a lot. There are also characters here who clearly stereotype. I mention this as a warning that what follows at times crosses that line between generalizations (helpful) and stereotypes (unhelpful/hurtful). Sometimes it is deliberate to make a point, other times I've made a mistake.

The point is, it is an important topic and one we should embrace if we're going to figure out how to work together effectively.

Several of the characters throughout these stories tend to drink too much and behave in questionable ways. Male-dominated work cultures and the "old boys club" mentality still exist. These are issues that need to be discussed more openly if progress is to be made. Colorful characters like these are a reality, and despite their behavior, we can learn from them. I also occasionally write out accents whether they are American, Taiwanese, Australian, or another. I do this to help bring out a character, not make fun of anyone. I also use humor, sarcasm, and occasional vulgarity, which many cross-cultural professionals advise against. I have ignored that advice.

Finally, there are a lot of stories here where people and companies would prefer to remain anonymous, so the names and details for most of these incidents have been changed to protect the guilty.

With that said, let's get on with this adventure...

Introduction

I'm in an overpriced global coffee shop chain in Singapore. The shop's products are the same as back home—the look, feel, and smell of the place is universal. For some, it's globalization at its finest. For others, it's a dystopian nightmare of bland corporate uniformity, yet for many it's just a coffee shop.

A small group of businesspeople place their order. Then one man—British, balding—throws a monkey wrench into the entire operation. He tries to order off the menu.

"You can only order from the menu," replies the barista.

"Of course, that's not a problem, just charge me for it. I'm supposed to dissolve this medicine into hot water, so I just need a cup of hot water," he said holding up a small white packet with a prescription stuck to it.

"Sorry, has to be from the menu."

"Mate," he says in a British way that means the barista is anything but his mate. He continues through slightly gritted teeth. "I'm happy to pay for it. I need to take this medicine."

"Cannot."

The British man is now *screaming on the inside.*

Screaming on the inside. It's a wonderful phrase to describe any moment of peak frustration where you are backed into a corner. In your mind, that corner has been forced by interaction that was entirely avoidable.

The British man would like to scream on the outside, but he's with his work colleagues and he's trying to hold it together.

Thankfully, a woman in his group interjects and addresses the barista. "He'll have a tea. Earl Gray. Please keep the tea bag on the side."

The barista smiles. This order can be processed. The hot water problem has been solved. His medicine can now be dissolved.

This example may sound trite—unless you're standing in line behind the man. And it may be trite, at least on the surface. But if you step back and think from a global perspective, the example suddenly becomes more meaningful, symbolic, and informative. At least, it did to me, and I think it might to you, too. It offers one of many subtle yet critical lessons about business in the global economy.

This book grew out of a few simple questions:

If I could go back a decade, what would I tell my younger, less gray-haired self as I was setting up a business in Asia—or anywhere outside of Europe or Japan? What are the warnings? What do I need to avoid? What advice would my younger self hear but then ignore?

The next question became, how would I explain this stuff to someone who hasn't gone through it yet? There are cultural differences across the globe that our senses pick up: language, food, rituals. But there are a lot more invisible differences our senses don't immediately register: unspoken rules, roles, beliefs, and values.

How do you explain to someone from the United States that the idea of individual liberty is not a universal value? Democracy? A lot of people on this planet don't believe in it. Equality? Meh. Privacy? Not here. You get the picture. There are people who may instead prioritize concepts like seniority—hierarchy—as a core tenet and who believe the group takes priority over any one individual. But a majority of business books, trainings and management ideas have been created in places like the US, where ideas such as individualism and equality are assumed. If a majority of the planet doesn't behave that way, what happens when a bunch of differing values come into contact? What happens when you apply pressure like tight deadlines or millions of dollars? Things get intense fast.

Take one example of how people communicate. It varies widely. For example, ask a New Yorker to borrow money and he may say no. While someone from London may respond "we'll see" and in Japan it may be a yes. The end answer in all three cases is the same. You aren't getting that money. Confusing, right? Nearly everyone thinks their way is the right way. They are all right. Globally, they are all wrong.

I take this personally because these issues nearly bankrupted my company, cost me and my clients millions of dollars, and drove me to the point where I was ready to give up and become a barista for the rest of my life.

All because I am an accidental business nomad.

My "10 years ago self" saw what looked like a great opportunity, and I jumped on it. And jumped where the opportunity was—Asia. My business quickly expanded across ten countries in four continents, and then I tried to force fit a uniform global standard onto clients who very much wanted and needed a local standard. The only thing faster than the growth was the collapse.

As I picked up the pieces from my own business, I started asking myself some hard questions. What happened? What went wrong? What would I do differently? Every answer had one common denominator. Culture. Culture affects businesses as they expand around the world. As I wrestled through this tricky topic, it became clear that many others were struggling with this as well. I soon saw my losses were nothing compared to other businesses. Some completely failed, while others muddled through it. A tiny few seemed to naturally figure things out.

As globalization continues to accelerate, more people are wrestling with similar challenges. Technology has taken businesses across borders, but bringing people together causes culture clashes to expand. Technology quickly erases geographical borders, but in many ways cultural borders become magnified.

Recently, I did a workshop with a team of executives from around the world, and we spent time talking about *beliefs* and *values*. Many companies have a *values statement* or something similar. What's yours? More important, how does a company have a values statement if people around the world don't share the same values? Or, suppose they share those values, but they *express* them differently?

Here's an example: a team agreed that *honesty* and *respect* were two core values that the company and their team held in high regard. Wonderful, you might say. You see? People around the world do share similar values. We are all one global village.

But wait, how do each of the people in that room *express* those values? How do you show respect? What does honesty mean?

One of the British managers spoke up. He led a global marketing team scattered across five continents. His company was launching a marketing campaign driving people to attend a coffee or tea meeting to learn more about his company's products. The plan was for all markets to launch the campaign at the same time to keep things organized and consistent. But he tried to be flexible from a cultural standpoint. Some countries prefer tea, others coffee—this is a cultural difference we can all see, and in this case, taste. Countries can choose. They would rewrite the invite accordingly.

Meanwhile, his Malaysian employee knows this plan won't work in Malaysia. But the employee goes along with it anyway. He doesn't speak up.

Why? Because he's honoring the core values—respect and honesty—set by the team. Where he comes from, it is disrespectful to challenge and push back on someone more senior. Showing respect is honest. His version of the value statement has been fulfilled.

But why won't the coffee or tea meeting work in Malaysia?

It's Ramadan. In Malaysia, most of the target audience can eat and drink only after the sun sets. Daylight is for fasting. Inviting people out for coffee or tea is not only a waste of time, it's showing a complete lack of understanding of local customs. If a company doesn't know about Ramadan, how would they know about helping local clients and their local challenges? The campaign is an embarrassment in Malaysia—an expensive embarrassment.

The British manager is screaming on the inside. Why didn't his Malaysian employee speak up? The manager thinks his employee is incompetent, useless. He broke the team's core values statement. What happened to honesty and respect? The manager is quietly putting a plan together to find a replacement for this team member.

Who's right here? Who's wrong?

This is one small and, yes, real example of misunderstandings that happen across global teams. Miscommunication also happens through the *lack* of communicating, like what happened here. Some theories help explain what's happening. We can look at ideas on how to overcome them as well, and we will do that in later chapters.

On a trip back to the United States recently, I brought up this Malaysia example during a workshop on behavioral profiling. Everyone in the room perked up. They were experiencing new and similar frustrations, not necessarily with Malaysia, but this story sounded a lot like the new challenges they were wrestling with in places like Russia, Brazil, India, China, and even the United Kingdom. In fact, they were having trouble defining the issues in the first place. The first conclusion is usually, "Well, this person doesn't know what he is doing," and, "People over there don't really 'get it.'"

In fact, the problem is the exact opposite. The person is doing what he or she has been culturally programmed to do. Cultures vary, and failing to understand or appreciate that fact is where problems start.

That is when it hit me. Situations like these are no longer isolated moments unique to a small group of expat managers. Cultural misunderstandings happen much more frequently today. Because of communication technology and the digital economy, global businesspeople no longer need a well-worn passport to work internationally. Understanding international communication isn't just for multinationals, start-ups, freelancers, or small businesses—everyone is now working across the planet. We're all global now. We're all foreigners.

Many of us have jumped at opportunities for global work adventures, while others have been more reluctant. Regardless, the global workforce is here, and it brings with it a new set of challenges.

You might think the large global companies that have done this for decades have figured it out. They have not. The ongoing collapse of distance has opened vast opportunities but also vast challenges for companies of all sizes. Some expensive challenges, some deadly, some stupidly funny.

There are many more *screaming on the inside* moments occurring. Understand what causes these situations, and you'll begin to crack the code of communicating globally. Fortunately, there are a lot of tools and ideas that can help, and we'll explore many of them in depth in the forthcoming pages. You'll figure out how to navigate these invisible global obstacles and how to build stronger relations that will help you to advance moments of true innovation. I have added a few tips at the end of each chapter as a starting point. Many of the concepts are simple, but actually doing them is hard and takes practice. Working globally can be wildly frustrating and overwhelming, but it is often these very moments that, if handled correctly can turn into great opportunities and unexpected bursts of innovation and creativity. We're all business nomads now, so let's figure this out together.

Chapter 1

Into the Den of
Slap Dragons

"Those who cannot change their minds cannot change anything."

—*George Bernard Shaw*

Businesses continue to lose a ton of money and opportunities overseas because they can't accept that their way may not always be the right way. The first step to succeed in a global environment is to realize that you don't know what you don't know. Only then will the world open up its opportunities.

REMEMBER THE FIRST time I walked into this bar about 15 years ago with a power adapter in my hand and thinking that while nothing else had gone well earlier in the day, I had a least figured out the power plug situation. My computer was out of battery, and the Singapore wall outlets didn't work with my American plug. I kept forgetting to bring an adapter with me and ended up buying several. To this day, I have baskets filled with the things. My baggy suit was drenched with sweat from wandering around in the tropical heat. I came to the bar to meet a guy named Stu, an Australian, living here in Singapore.

Overheated and underwhelmed with my current work situation, it had been a frustrating day. I discovered that the team of 10 callers I had hired a few weeks earlier had not made a single phone call in the past five days. Their job was to cold call thousands of companies and try to sell tech products from a number of different clients. They should have been averaging 100 calls a day—at least! The reason for the lack of calls was apparently my fault. I had given them unclear instructions when I had asked them to hold off calling for one specific client. They interpreted that as holding off calling for *all* clients. The team leader did not understand why I was so upset when I arrived in the office to find the group doing no work. How did this happen? I didn't know, but I was convinced I had hired a bunch of idiots. After complaining about the situation to a friend, he put me in touch with Stu.

I found two guys sitting at a small table in the crowded pub. They introduced themselves as Stu and Smitty. I had told Stu earlier that drinks were on me, and now it looked like I was covering his friend as well.

This would be the first of many after-work meetups, where people working for global companies would get together, compare war stories, commiserate, celebrate, and generally try to figure out how to work across a shrinking planet—or at least get drunk trying. It was a lesson in global leadership, barroom style.

I ordered three beers for the table and the waiter replied, "It's one-for-one." This was a happy hour promotion found throughout Singapore and other nearby countries.

"OK. As I said, we'll have three beers, please." I was slightly annoyed with the waiter. After all, it had been a long day, and now I had to decode whatever "one-for-one" meant. I looked at my new colleagues for confirmation I was doing the right thing, but they stared back at me stone-faced.

I hadn't been in the region long but was beginning to realize I was in over my head. Things were different than I had expected, but it was hard to define what those differences were. Sure, the cars driving on the other side of the road, the languages, and the power sockets were different. These things that could be seen and heard were easy, but they weren't the real obstacles to working in other parts of the world. I was beginning to realize that it was the invisible stuff that caused the real problems.

* * *

I didn't understand at the time, but this meetup was intended to help me understand these invisible things.

"Welcome to the land of grizzled and bitter expats," Stu said in his thick Australian accent. "Hopefully we can give you some pointers to make life a little easier."

Stu was well liked around town. His parents moved to Sydney from Taiwan before he was born. He grew up in Australia and was as Australian as it gets. His passion for watching cricket was matched only by his love of Vegemite. He has been known to lecture his foreign friends on why the Australian band Midnight Oil is one of the most important bands ever. "Evah." A few years ago, his company gave him a major promotion and sent him to Singapore to run their Asia operations. There were people more qualified, but Stu was of

Asian heritage. And this was the reason he got the job, because his corporate bosses thought he looked the part. "Funny thing is, I know a little bit about Taiwan because of my parents, but that place is 2,000 miles away from Singapore and a totally different market. My Asian looks didn't help much once I got here."

The waiter returned with six pints of beer. "Um, I only ordered three," I said. "One-for-one," responds the waiter, "three beers," pointing at the six glasses before disappearing into the crowd.

I remember staring at the table, dumbfounded, while Smitty dove in for his two pints and Stu laughed. Annoyed, I asked, "What the hell does 'one-for-one' mean?"

"It means 'two for the price of one,' mate," said Smitty in a gravelly East London accent. After an unnaturally long pull of his beer he continued, "You ordered three drinks. Since it's one-for-one, that means you get two of everything. It's just how things are done around here."

"Why would he pour us six beers? There are three of us sitting here," I was screaming on the inside. "Your first lesson has begun!" Stu raised his glass to make a toast. "I wish all our mistakes were this tasty!"

With my six pints, I had stumbled into a lesson on communicating across cultures. Regardless of what words get said, the important thing is what the other person *perceives*. In my case, the waiter perceived that I understood the meaning of one-for-one. Communication breakdowns happen between everyone, even people who know each other well. Misunderstandings multiply between people who come from entirely different places. These can lead to big mistakes. Or in this case, tasty ones.

Smitty *was* grizzled and he was nearly finished with his first pint already. He was a project manager for a giant construction company, and he had been in Asia forever. He sounded as if he had been in this bar all afternoon, which was not going to help his sporadic bouts of gout. Smitty was the guy in sketchy bars, with beer dribbling down his faded Hawaiian shirt, watching the world go by. But he was no slouch. During the workweek he was a high-functioning employee, respected by most of his colleagues and, as I would learn later, one of the most dependable people in the region. Smitty has seen it all and done it all. He knew how to get things done across the region. He was a doer.

Smitty managed people all around the region, from Australia to India. Locals around the planet get frustrated with foreign managers who come in and do things their own way, but Smitty wasn't like that. He watched what was going on around him and learned from it. Most important, he got results. The way he got results wasn't always pretty. The way he solved problems wouldn't get written up in business school case studies. But he made things happen, and when executives came in trying to apply foreign solutions to local problems, he was the one who kept things from imploding.

Locals in Singapore have a nickname for Western executives. They're called "seagulls." These were big, often white birds who flap down from out of the sky, make a lot of noise, crap all over the place, and then fly away. I had certainly made a few messes already, largely because I was clueless. But I had plenty of company.

The four phases of learning to work globally

The first lesson I had to learn when working in Asia was that I didn't know what was going on. It took me a while to realize how little I knew. Thankfully, I wasn't alone. This was a difficult first lesson to accept. In fact, some never accept it. It was only when something bad happened that people realized they were in over their heads. Here is the learning curve everyone goes through when working in foreign markets:

Phase one: You have no idea what is going on and you don't realize it—so you do things the way you've always done them. Business as usual. This is what I had done with my local team when I told them to stop working on the newest campaign. I handled that situation the way I would have back in the United States.

Phase two: You realize you have no idea what is going on because what you're doing isn't working.

Phase three: You begin to learn how to handle situations in new ways. You practice, you screw up, you try again.

Phase four: You figure it out and can navigate any global situation. One-for-one's all night long.

After my first month in Singapore, I was firmly stuck in phase one. I had learned how to build teams back in the United States that were effective, and I was here to do the same in Asia. I thought that my way was the right way because it had worked back home. That's why I was here, and that's why clients were hiring me. As I chatted with Stu and Smitty over our beers, I began to realize I was out of my depth in Asia. That meeting marked my transition from phase one to phase two. I was reluctantly beginning to understand I didn't know what I was doing. The more stubborn and headstrong the person, the harder it is to break out of phase one.

My pride was hurt. I found myself lost and confused, officially in that second phase. Not only that, I was despondent. The biggest irony of working overseas became clear—the leadership skills that got me here were now somehow causing me to fail in these new markets.

Stu and Smitty were embedded in phase three, learning and figuring out how to work across diverse situations. The people sitting around that expat bar were all working through these challenges. I would learn that many of the people with experience working overseas did not know how to properly explain what they were going through. Instead, it turned into rough versions of barroom anecdotes and on-the-fly tips and tricks. Over the years I would discover a better way.

Phase three was all about collecting tools and techniques to navigate these challenges. Phase four was mastery. This was where a person could use these tools without having to think about them. They could adjust to situations automatically. To this day, I have only met one person who has reached this phase. His name is Axel, and you will meet him later.

The people here were all players in a game of globalization that has accelerated during the past few decades. We came overseas because we were looking for something. We were chasing a dream of winning globally. Thousands of companies have expanded overseas during the past few years, racing to get their piece of the growing global pie and spending tons of money in the process. From the largest multinationals down to the start-ups, everyone seemed to be going global. This meant more people from more parts of the world were doing business together and often, they realized that there were important differences that needed to get sorted out in order to make things work.

Global success requires having grit and enjoying the ride

Everyone bought into the idea that the world had suddenly opened for business. In many ways it had. We thought that business was done the same way no matter the country; we had been told the world was flat. Yes, technology opened borders and investment led to increased levels of global integration, but those who ventured over the horizon to new markets found something else that turned out to be much more complicated. What should have been straightforward assignments turned into mazes of miscommunication and cultural mishaps to which no one seemed to have the map.

Who wins, who loses? What are the traits of success when working in these fast-paced multicultural environments? I noticed two things right away: those who lasted and who were succeeding were tough. They had grit. Sometimes that expressed itself in less-than-politically correct ways, like Smitty. More on him and his gang later. The second trait was that they enjoyed the adventure. Those who were simply in it for the money or took all the stress of global work too seriously were usually the ones who went home empty-handed.

I didn't know it at the time, but building a roadmap to help companies and people get through this cross-cultural maze would turn into my main area of focus. How can people work effectively across a complex planet where invisible communication and working styles vary so widely? My adventure in discovering these answers was just beginning.

In the bar that night I described my business plan to Stu and Smitty. I helped companies from a wide range of industries sell more of their products and services by getting them in front of new prospects. This involved mostly cold calling but also emailing and using newer online tools to help companies sell more of their stuff. Clients had started to turn their attention to Asian markets and I had pitched myself as the guy who could help them grow around this emerging region. The marketing and sales work I had done in the United States could now be done across Asia. What should have been a plug-and-play game plan that had worked in the US was already failing miserably here in Singapore. My team of callers was not making calls, and I had begun to realize that what I had promised my clients now seemed almost impossible.

One client I had overpromised was Texas Joe. I called him "Texas Joe" because that is where he was from and from where he had no interest in leaving. Joe ran a company that sold software to banks, and somehow he landed a deal with a local bank in Singapore. This got him excited about selling into more Asian banks, and he found and hired me to help him do it.

Joe didn't know anything about Asia, and he didn't care to learn. To him, business was business in any and every part of the world. If a bunch of Asian countries were growing their markets like crazy, then that was all he needed to know. Texas Joe believed the world would bend to his wishes if he pushed hard enough.

I had spoken with him a few nights earlier. Even with less than a week of experience in Asia, I knew more than Joe. He wanted me to send his marketing brochures out to all of the banks in Malaysia, Singapore, and Hong Kong. The problem was that his material was covered in baseball images and phrases. "Cover your bases," "hit it out of the park," that kind of thing. I tried to explain that people in these countries don't play baseball and that the message would not work. That's when he got frustrated. "Slap a frigging dragon on it and that will make it Asian." That statement so eloquently captured Joe's ignorance. Putting aside the fact that it showed an appalling lack of understanding of Asians and demonstrated a truly awful level of stereotyping. (How might Joe feel if someone suggested, "Slap a frigging eagle on it and that will make it American"?) More than anything, though, it showed ignorance. I began thinking of him and anyone else who ignored cultural differences as *slap dragons*. Joe didn't care about what he didn't know, and that was an expensive combination, as I was about to learn.

Against my better judgment, I did as Joe asked. I slapped a dragon on it.

Sitting on a plastic bedsheet—at the time I was living in the cheapest hotel in town—I had found an image of a dragon online and I slapped it over the baseball players. It looked…good enough. So, it was blasted out to banks across Asia.

It was not a home run.

Texas Joe fired me a few weeks later based on the poor results. This was my first *slap dragon* moment, but I was creating new ones by the day.

Stu shook his head, unimpressed with my marketing efforts. This was not an effective example of localizing products. Smitty just laughed—clearly, he was familiar with Texas Joe–types who rocked up in Asia with utter confidence and zero knowledge. "Guys like that don't understand the region," he said. "If they did, they wouldn't be making such fools of themselves."

Smitty threw out an idea. "You get the slap dragon guy to come visit and take him to a certain bar nearby where the ladies there are *nice and friendly*." He made crude gestures with his hands. "Then, once he gets nice and comfortable with one of the ladies—and I mean *nice* and friendly—you take him aside and whisper in his ear, 'You just had your hands all over a *guy*, you muppet!'" He laughed at his ingenuity. "Guys like Joe don't understand the region. If they did, they wouldn't have their hand up men's skirts! *That* is how you get the guys back home to understand!"

This was by no means a Smitty original, and it was not barroom bluster. It was in fact, a common maneuver pulled on visiting executives. The varied nightlife scene meant it wasn't always easy to guess the gender or sex of the person next to you at the bar, and locals were often more than happy to help teach cocky Westerners a lesson about the big, complex world. The message was clear: *Don't assume you know how things work around here*. This was the kind of advice that didn't make it into many "how-to-do-business-overseas" books. But Smitty was just getting started. I would later learn that Smitty loved messing with Americans who were new in town because they tended to have less overseas experience than other Westerners. Yes, Americans were "seagulls," but he thought of them more as "fish" because when they weren't making noise, they were swimming around in circles, clueless. Even when they learned something, they forgot it immediately. I tried not to take this personally.

"Maybe I should tell him how we lost half a million euros trying to bribe a company up in Thailand?" Smitty said, looking at Stu, who was enjoying the banter.

Good bribery stories were the low-hanging fruit of expat lore, and I would learn later that like so many things, it was not a black-and-white issue. Standard business practices in one part of the world were illegal in others, and global organizations were constantly dancing between the various realities. Smitty's story served as a good introduction. A handful of contractors and government types in the middle-of-nowhere Thailand needed some extra encouragement to get a building project approved. Smitty was tasked with paying these guys off. But the details proved devilish. How does someone actually pay a bribe? How do they get past their company's compliance department, which needs to see documentation of all cash, especially if they are a publicly traded company? How was it done across borders? Does the cash actually go into a bag?

Smitty was up for the challenge. He worked his contacts inside his company to see if anything like this had been done before. That was met with laughter, because of course it had been done before. An offshore shell company had been set up years earlier for just such activities. There was even a Word document sitting on a company server with step-by-step details of how to pay bribes. He simply had to follow the instructions. He hired a local Thai to deliver a bag—yes there was an actual bag—of cash. The guy ran off with the money. So, he found a second guy and a second bag and a second half a million euros and tried again. And that worked.

"You lost a million euros if you include the bribe," I said, trying to redeem myself from my slap dragon project.

"Mate, the million did *exactly* what it was meant to. Best investment we made up there. If those bastards were smarter, they'd have asked us for more!"

This was the shady way of getting things done. Large multinationals all had their own Smittys operating silently within their ranks. In most parts of the so-called emerging markets, the shadow economies were more efficient than the legal channels. In India, for example, it was called "black-and-white money." Paying the black money is usually faster and easier than paying the white, legal money. In the world according to Smitty, it was the rule of *power*, not the rule of *law*, that mattered.

But Smitty's bribery story wasn't helping me with my people problems. Here in squeaky-clean Singapore, I wasn't about to bribe my way out of my situation. So Smitty changed tactics.

"Now, China is a different world. Our global CEO was being driven to some godforsaken place to visit a manufacturing plant, and they got into a traffic accident and a local guy died. Just ran the poor bastard over. That kind of thing can end a company and land you in jail. But we had our well-paid local guide who sorted the whole thing out on the spot." The CEO supposedly watched from his car as the body was buried right there on the side of the road. "And that was the end of it."

I didn't know how to respond to any of this. This conversation had turned dark quickly.

Thai bribery, Chinese hit-and-runs, one-for-one. This really was a trial by fire.

Smitty turned serious and raised his near-empty second glass for a toast. "Welcome to the jungle, mate. You've got a lot to learn."

Speeding up by slowing down

There's an old joke where one fish asks another fish, "How's the water?" and the second fish replies, "What's water?"

I had landed in an unfamiliar pond and quickly realized that what was normal to me was not normal in other parts of the world. It was *culture shock*, and psychologists who study the phenomenon suggest it can take more than a year to work through the common phases of adjustment. It was highly likely these psychologists had never lived abroad, because in reality it took much longer.

Some people move through the learning phases faster than others. Some companies muddle through them, others don't invest the time, money, and effort needed to survive the learning curve. Many leaders can't break out of their mental programming and see the world from wildly different angles. Few talk about it openly. Who wants to admit they are a *slap dragon*?

But there were answers to these problems. Stu and his company were one example. They seemed to have cracked the mystery, navigating the cross-cultural roadblocks that slow down or end so many other organizations. Their year-over-year double-digit growth was part of the proof.

Promoted based on a faulty assumption that his ethnicity equalled cultural understanding, Stu had been growing a successful business, winning bigger and better deals. Stu hired locals and he spent a ton of time learning about what they did in their last job. While most managers jumped right into their expectations for the future, he focused on the past. The reason he did this was to understand how the new hire got things done. He asked them about the times things went well and the times things did not go well. Once he had a clear picture of the new employee's background, he could explain things in ways that made sense to that person. He had personalized the new hire process. Time consuming, but effective.

For Stu, the wins were slow to come at first, and there were a lot of growing pains. His shop kept on top of problems quickly and did something others did not: they learned from their mistakes and spoke openly about them. On top of that, there was a company culture of brutal honesty.

"We hired Stu because he knew what he was doing and seemed to get along with people easily," his CEO told me later when I began researching global growth success stories. "So I got that right when I hired him. Then I sent him to Singapore because he looked Asian, and that was pretty stupid. So I get half marks."

That's some pretty honest self-assessment.

They also got lucky being in the right place at the right time, but, more than luck, the company gave itself enough time to figure things out. "I didn't know what else to do, so I just kept asking everyone questions all the time," said Stu. "And that got other people asking questions, and we built this office where it was OK to ask questions. This prevented a lot of issues."

Stu didn't worry about how to *grow*, he was focused on how to manage growth in a world that was *shrinking*. He seemed to naturally grasp the fact that when people got pulled closer together, differences in working styles became more apparent. One person may want detailed instructions on a task, while another person might want the flexibility to do things their own way. Some people got loud, while others went quiet. Some were used to a workspace where the boss was always right, and others were accustomed to telling the boss what to do. Stu somehow understood this, and he was good at heading off problems before they started.

How do people new to working with people from different parts of the world avoid the mistakes I had made? How do they succeed like Stu? Was it possible to avoid these cross-cultural mishaps, or was the new global workforce destined to fall into the same mistakes again and again? Was there a shortcut to being globally ready? How do you show someone something invisible they don't want to see? How do you tell a fish about the water?

Adaptor

Back in the bar, I was still confused by what happened with the beer order. How does ordering three beers turn into six?

I clearly remember blaming the waiter. He was an idiot, like the program manager who let my team sit around doing nothing for a week.

Stu jumped in, pointing at the drinks, "This is the same thing as your work problems. You've got a team that is not calling and another client telling you to slap dragons on things to make them Asian. Your communication is not working, and you are working off of a play-book from back home."

I felt a bit defensive. My plan was to replace the program manager who allowed the callers to do nothing with someone else. "And what happens when the new program manager does something you don't like? Are you going to replace that person too? How about the waiter, should he get fired? How about the bartender who poured the beers? How many people are you going to replace until you find someone who you like? There's one person responsible in these situations, my friend, and it's you."

This was tough advice that I did not want to hear. It was beginning to dawn on me that he was right, but it didn't make things any easier. "If I were you," Stu added, "I would slow everything down. Before you come in changing things, take time to learn what is going on, how things work here. Get to know the people in the office." He picked up my power plug adapter. "This," he said, "you can't jam your tiny US plug into a wall outlet here and expect it to work. You need one of these. It's the same with how you handle the people. You have to learn how to adapt."

I was being smacked and beaten out of phase one.

"Here's one simple trick that I guarantee will make your life easier: listen to people differently than you ever have before." Stu elaborated, "When someone tells you something, toss it back in the form of a question to make sure you understand clearly and do it all the time."

Smitty summoned the waiter and gave an example. "Here's how you do it. The next time the waiter says it's one-for-one, repeat it back as a question. 'When you say one-for-one, can you explain that?' That's how you get what you want here."

I told him I'd work on it.

"No mate, you have to practice. Now!" he smiled widely as he summoned the waiter. I had been suckered into ordering another round.

"You guys are bastards," I said, smiling, raising my glass as a toast to my new friends.

I walked unsteadily out of the bar later that night thinking about the conversation. There was a lot to process. When my new team stopped working for five days because of unclear instructions, I had taken the critical first step of realizing that I did not know what I was up against. Clearly, working with overseas teams required new ways of approaching problems, and the world was not going to change to suit my way of doing business. I didn't yet know exactly how to adjust, but the realization alone was a critical step.

Then there were these two wildly different personalities giving advice. Stu was telling me I had to adjust by slowing everything down, learning more about my teammates. Smitty was telling me if I wanted to get things done, I'd need to lose my naïveté because rules were different across the world. In their own ways, they were both telling me to drop my preconceived notions and open my mind to new ways of getting things done. Furthermore, I'd need to actively question everything. *Active listening*, as Stu mentioned— throwing a statement back to the speaker in the form of a question— was one of the easiest and most effective speaking techniques to clarify unclear statements. This was a critical tool for helping see the invisible obstacles lurking across the globe. It was comforting knowing there were people out there willing to help, or at least trying to help. Unfortunately, their guidance came in bits and pieces. I was going to have to struggle through all this. I didn't know it at the time, but I was at the early stages of piecing together a series of tools that would help people quickly learn how to adapt around the world.

Outside the bar, I found an available taxi and I opened the passenger door. Wrong. It was the driver's door. Cars drive on the other side in Singapore. Even with the things I could see it was hard to change behavior. This was going to be one hell of a ride.

Survival Guide Tips:

✔ To localize effectively, don't be a slap dragon. Take the time to adapt products, services and mindsets. Start by acknowledging what you don't know and question past assumptions about what you think is the right way to do things.

✔ To communicate effectively around the planet, use active listening. Rephrase or paraphrase anything that is unclear to better understand what is being said.

Chapter 2

Ghostbusters
and Gweilos

"All you need in this life is ignorance and confidence, and then
    success is sure."

—*Mark Twain*

Many companies approach overseas growth by faking it till
they make it. One of the consequences of this poorly thought
out approach is that culture clashes happen quickly and often.
People from all over the world wrestle with these new people
challenges. This chapter looks at some of those examples.

SINGAPORE IS AN island nation that is rated number one in the world by the World Bank for its ease of doing business. More and more companies have a presence in Singapore because it is a safe and attractive place to run an Asian operation.[1] It has one of the best airports in the world, with state-of-the-art infrastructure throughout the island. The skyline looks like *the future*. A bright, clean, safe future.

I thought about these things while sitting in my "hotel" that I had recently learned, rented rooms by the hour. This sort of hotel didn't offer internet access, but I found a nearby unsecured wifi connection that kept me going through the night. This was yet another Skype call with a client from the United States who didn't seem to understand time zones and the fact that it was 1 a.m. here. She was talking about her cat. Hopefully the noise-canceling headphones did their job because these walls were thin. I thought about my housing situation—the plastic sheets, the super-cheap rates, the geckos zigzagging across the walls catching bugs, and the small, dirty window that looked out at the side of a grungy building.

This was not the international business adventure I had thought I was getting into, and I was quickly learning that many things in the global business world were not what they seemed. But I had made my plastic-covered bed, and I was determined to lie in it.

In one of the last scenes in the original *Ghostbusters* movie, Dan Aykroyd's character meekly approaches a vixen spirit. The spirit asks Aykroyd in a demonic voice if he is a god. Aykroyd looks at Bill Murray's character, who nods and gives a little fist pump as if to say, "you got this." Aykroyd replies quietly, "No." The spirit answers, "Then die!" and zaps the Ghostbusters with lightning. As they recover, a third Ghostbuster played by Ernie Hudson declares, "When someone asks you if you are a god, you say YES!"

This advice was known as the Ghostbusters Principle. It's another way of saying "fake it till you make it." It's a kind of overconfident optimism that suggests you'll find a way to figure things out in real time or get fried trying. It takes a bit of this attitude to expand business overseas. Of course, there are limits to our omnipotence, so the trick is to find some type of balance that keeps things from falling apart. As the woman on the phone droned on, the Ghostbusters Principle floated through my thoughts, and I was reminded of how I ended up here.

Back in the United States a few months earlier, I had been asked by a client if I could deliver a marketing program across their Asia offices. They needed a team to work the phones, handling inbound phone calls and chats, and call prospects in a half-dozen languages, all with the goal of selling more of their client's technology hardware. They did not know where to start, so could I do it for them? I didn't think much about it and simply said yes.

Quickly realizing this was a big project, I made the 24-hour commute to Singapore to figure out how to get it done. It became clear this would not be simple, and a few round trips later, I decided to buy a one-way ticket and hunker down in a cheap hotel to figure out my next move. None of this was planned. I had become a business nomad by accident.

This project epitomized the new world of globalization. A tech giant outsourced a critical piece of marketing and sales to an agency who outsourced it to me. I then outsourced it to someone else. There were more people managing this tenuous supply chain than doing any of the work.

The agency in the United States that hired me was a publicly traded company. They already updated their website announcing they had a new Asia Pacific (often called "APAC") office in Singapore. That was me. On a Skype call. Pirating wifi while sitting on a plastic sheet whose history I dared not contemplate. It seemed there were a lot of us applying the Ghostbuster Principle.

This mindset was important in the early years of the new millennium, when businesses began rapidly expanding around the world. This was a new phase of globalization where companies of all shapes and sizes, one way or another, were extending their footprint. Some were chasing cheaper materials and products, others were looking to cut costs by moving "non-business critical" operations to cheaper parts of the world (more on this in the next chapter), and many had their eyes on the biggest prize of all: the newly emerging Asian middle class. China, the Middle Kingdom, has a middle class roughly the size of the entire population of the United States and growing. India has approximately the same number of people as China (if they haven't overtaken them as the most populated country, they will soon), with a ballooning middle class as well. The smaller ASEAN (Association of Southeast Asian Nations) countries (a group of 10 nations near China) will add another 500 million middle-class consumers by 2030.[2] Added together, we are talking about more than a billion new consumers. As Parag Khanna, an international relations specialist, wrote in his book *The Future is Asian*, "Asia will forever be home to more people than the rest of the world combined. They are now speaking. Prepare to see the world from the Asian point of view." This, of course, was the problem. Slap dragons were descending.

Rising tide, leaky boats

During the first few weeks of my new project, the shine was beginning to fade from the façade. Doing business in different parts of the world turned out to be harder than I'd expected. I had already made a mistake by telling the calling team to "stop calling" for one client, causing all the calling programs to grind to a halt. Along with communication issues, there were constant headaches slowing down progress. There seemed to be a holiday in one country or another every week and countless other unexpected human resource obstacles. Military service in Singapore is compulsory for all male citizens, and until the age of 40, they are required to take two weeks off work each year for ongoing training. It seemed customary to make this known to employers at the very last moment. Unexpected costs both visible and invisible began adding up quickly.

Despite these headaches, new projects came flying in as more and more companies wanted a piece of the Asian pie. The requests were as diverse and unpredictable as the region itself, and I kept saying yes!

Can you represent me over in Hong Kong?
Yes.
Can you get me a database of every telecom provider in Vietnam?
Erm, sure.
Can you help out my team in the Philippines?
Why not?
Can your team handle inbound sales inquiries in Mandarin, Thai and Bahasa?
Absolutely. Whatever Bahasa was.
What do you know about tractors?
Tractors? Tons, let's do it.

New clients came on board quickly. The idea of having a sales and marketing unit operating in Asia was an attractive offer for many companies who wanted to fake it till they made it. However, there were a lot of companies faking it and not many actually making it, which meant a lot of poorly thought out expansion plans were taking place and causing more problems than they were solving. One company selling farming equipment learned quickly that not all markets were created equal. When a company tried to explain how much more efficient their tractors were than manual labor, prospects in Indonesia politely declined. In a country with no health insurance or workers compensation, and a near-limitless supply of low-wage workers, tractors didn't actually cut costs. It was not uncommon to see fields being mowed by dozens of people using weed-whackers or hedge clippers. Sometimes people were cheaper than machines. The return on investment (ROI) calculations companies were using had to be completely rebuilt.

I was one small part of this problem because I kept saying yes to anyone wanting to enter these markets. I wasn't versed in Indonesia's tractor situation, for example, so my ghostbuster approach ended up creating some expensive lessons. When it comes to getting into the global game, yes, go for it, but do your homework first.

It was easy to get caught up in the momentum, and Singapore made it easy to set up shop. Here, government agencies responsible for approving the formation of new companies would send their approvals via text message, virtually unheard of from most public sector bureaucracies. They were making it easy to fake it.

Say a company decides that its product or service will sell like crazy in markets around the world. They might want to establish a sales office in that market. Maybe, before they do that, they want to test the waters by hiring a company that is already there to do the heavy lifting. Being *that company* is exactly what I had promised these clients. They were some of the easiest wins—none of these companies knew anyone in Asia, and they were all feeling the pressure to begin operating in the region. My clients knew I was starting up myself, but the push was on and they needed to show momentum. To them, I was better than nothing. In fact, I was ideal. As an American, I sounded like them and shared their approach to business, which made me easier to relate to.

Over the years, these projects gave me insights into hundreds of business expansion plans. Some were flimsy, quick-hit approaches, some were well-thought-out frameworks, and others were spend-whatever-it-takes strategies. They all took unexpected twists and turns, but within all the plans there was one consistent variable that kept everyone off-balance: people.

Globalizing business was no longer just about giant cargo ships moving goods from one place to the other, it had become human. Everyone was trying to figure out who they were suddenly working with across the planet. Who were they selling to? Who were they collaborating with? Who were their new colleagues? And everyone shared the same assumption that things would be business as usual, but usual according to whom? At this point in my adventure, I had created an illusion of competency and convinced my clients I understood what was going on. I had positioned myself as the one who could overcome these obstacles and accelerate growth. Now I had to deliver.

Outsourcing to local companies was OK, but I wanted more control and more of the upside. So I signed a lease for an apartment as well as for an office space. No more plastic sheets. No more faking it. It was time to start making things happen.

The call center business is pretty much a numbers game. To generate one good lead, a caller needs to talk to 10 to 15 people. Because many people won't answer their phone, this can take 80 to 100 dials a day. It took a good deal of effort, and that is why leads aren't cheap. Clients pay hundreds, if not thousands, of dollars for a single good lead. It was worth it to them if enough of these leads turned into high-paying clients.

The new office was what locals called a "shop house," a colorful colonial-era house that had been converted into commercial space, with stores and restaurants on the ground level and offices above. I had created what looked like a real workplace, filled with IKEA furniture. But there was not a lot of "work" taking place. Unfortunately, my newly hired team of cold callers averaged 15 calls *a day*, whereas I needed closer to 100 for this venture to work. A good caller could call as many prospects in *one hour* as my team called all day. And they could do it for seven or eight hours straight. I had hired a room full of locals with a bit of sales experience the same way I had back in Boston, but things were not working the same way here.

With the entire business based on simple calling metrics, the math was dire. I tried to incentivize the callers with extra pay if they hit their numbers and created accelerator bonuses if they overachieved, but nothing worked. I was not alone. Across the region, dozens of CEOs and vice presidents of sales told me they were having the same problem. Their salespeople were not making enough sales calls.

Once again, things were different than what I was used to.

Bad language

Jing Yi was the first project manager the company hired in Singapore. Her résumé was perfect. Coming from a prestigious school with good grades and a lot of extracurricular activities, she had spent five years after university in a few large firms managing local teams. I asked the usual interview questions to which she gave good answers. I told her I would be traveling a lot due to regional projects, so she would be leading a team on her own. She looked at me like I needed to get over myself because she knew what she was doing and wouldn't need me. That was exactly the answer I wanted. I hired her on the spot.

What happened after that was very different. Jing Yi did anything to avoid conflict. She avoided me at every turn. If an upset client asked her questions over the phone, she failed to provide any real answers. Instead, she would promise to solve the problem soon, but never followed up. This made difficult situations worse. If she finally did respond, it was via email, and she appeared devoid of any emotion or understanding of why the client was upset.

Making things harder, our clients were using software that could track everything we did. Our team would log in and work out of systems that clients could review at any time. This was important because it gave nearly full transparency to what our team was or, in our case, was not doing. I traveled frequently and often found my email filled with messages from clients questioning our low numbers of calls.

CLIENT: *Jing Yi, I logged into the system last night and saw that our two callers only made a combined 19 calls yesterday. Please let us know if there's any problem with the data, or if the team is having trouble navigating the system. These call volumes are unusually low.*

CLIENT: *Jing Yi, I didn't hear back from you on the note below. Can you please update me as it seems the call volumes today are lower than yesterday when I emailed you?*

JING YI: *Hi—our team is excited to be working with you. Please note that one of the callers was on MC* (this expression was not explained to the client, but it meant the employee was out sick) *today, and tomorrow is [one of many holidays], so work will resume next Monday. Best regards, Jing Yi*

The client was, rightly so, furious. It seemed the more upset that I or the client got, the quieter Jing Yi became. That made things worse. It was a nasty cycle, and I did not realize that my approach of confronting her about each of these issues directly was also making it worse.

Managing challenging employees was of course nothing new, but the problems coming out of Singapore were different from those in the United States. They varied elsewhere as well. I had a friend based in Brazil whom I had met at a call center event years earlier, and we kept in touch and compared notes on our challenges. He had the same problem getting results but for very different reasons. His project manager *fought* with her clients when they criticized her team's work. She yelled and screamed, and when she got upset, she would sometimes disappear for hours. On other occasions, he had trouble getting her to stick around the office—suddenly, she was getting along with the same client she had been fighting with days earlier, and she was spending all her time at the client's office. We both wished we had a little bit of each other's problems. I would soon learn there were helpful ways to better understand these behaviors and how to respond to them. For now, I was muddling through.

To keep the office funded, I took on consulting projects where I acted as a sales or marketing person for several Western companies unwilling or hesitant to fully invest in an Asian-based office.

Tractors, anyone? My name was on half a dozen different business cards. I hit the road, trying to solve problems or soothe clients from airport lounges and anywhere with a strong enough Internet connection. Everyone back in Singapore seemed to work even less when the boss was not around. But I was stuck because my own contracting jobs were the only thing keeping the call center open.

When I did make it to the office, my attempts to work with Jing Yi on the client communication issues went nowhere. Our relationship was formal, but I tried to keep things friendly. We spent little time together and when we did meet, we focused only on business. My expectation was that because she was an experienced team leader, she could handle her work and would reach out to me if anything was unclear or if she needed help. Otherwise, I assumed things were going fine. I was admittedly distracted trying to keep new projects coming in while traveling each week, and I didn't take any time to properly get to know her. After a few months, it seemed all our interactions were exercises in handling upset clients.

I would explain something and then ask, "Does that make sense?" She would tell me she understood but then go back to the exact behavior I was trying to correct. I was trying to use active listening as Stu had suggested, but it wasn't working, or, more likely, I wasn't doing it right. Every additional question I asked, I got a yes, but it didn't seem to mean yes.

Not only was I unable to effectively help my project manager, I couldn't figure out how to get the team to hit the phones. Motivational speeches, individual bonus incentives, and other techniques that worked for me back in the states fell on deaf ears. Yet for every client we lost due to poor performance, it seemed as if two new clients appeared, willing to replace them. We grew, despite our performance issues. The growth provided a reason to downplay the operational challenges. This, it turned out, was happening all around.

Many other Western companies were having similar problems managing local hires around the region. They would hire someone, fire them because of poor performance, and hire a Westerner with whom they felt more comfortable. This happened over and over again. In fact, this was how I won a number of clients. Sometimes it seemed as if we were just a bunch of Westerners doing deals with each other on this far-away continent.

High failure rates of cross-border mergers

This wasn't a one-way street, because local companies were also struggling when they hired Westerners. Often, within months, they would end up going their separate ways. I spoke with several frustrated Europeans and Australians who had either quit or been fired from local companies. The stories about inflexible management and unwillingness to try new things were common. One Singaporean company that bought an Australian company ended up replacing all the top Australians after the first few months of the acquisition. Another well-known Chinese firm acquired a German company and after letting go of all the Western leaders, declared they were implementing a "superior" 996 work schedule where employees were to work from 9 a.m. to 9 p.m. six days a week. The new management nearly lost all the employees and, after months of confusion, had to backtrack on all their proposed changes. This company tried to insert a Chinese approach overseas with disastrous consequences. This wasn't just a Western company problem. Everyone thought their way of doing things was the best. Recent studies suggest that mergers and acquisitions have between a 50 to 90 percent chance of failure.[3] The underlying problems almost always came back to the same thing: people and, specifically, culture clash.

It did not make sense. Was one group somehow better than the other? Why were Western companies having trouble managing locals? If Westerners were so good, why were successful local companies not hiring Westerners like crazy? The local companies seemed to be doing just fine. It was as if two worlds existed in parallel: East and West. It seemed that when their paths crossed, the likelihood of failure increased. What big piece of the puzzle was everyone missing? Many foreign managers would shrug their shoulders and announce that "people here just don't know what they are doing." The problem with that statement was the *people here* part. Foreign managers were saying this same thing *everywhere*. Something else was going on.

One Singaporean business contact agreed that people here didn't know what they were doing, but he was referring to the *foreign managers*. James Lee would meet me for morning walks and talk about business ideas. He provided a wonderful alternative viewpoint to how I was thinking about my team's problems. I first met James, an executive at a large HR consulting firm, at a networking event where he embraced me like an old friend. I went along with it for a few minutes until he realized his mistake. Clapping me on the shoulder he said, "So sorry, ah!" James had worked with a revolving door of Western managers and confused me with someone from his firm. Not at all embarrassed, he leaned in and whispered, "You Westerners all look alike! You know the movie *Oceans 11*? I could not watch. Everyone looked the same and I didn't know who's who!" I liked him immediately.

James did not have a lot of answers as to why Westerners could not get a higher level of performance from their employees, but his perspective was helpful because he was willing to share a very different way of seeing the world. From his point of view, foreigners were the problem, and if they didn't like the work ethic here, which he believed was stronger than in the West, they should leave. "We have the highest test scores in the world. We have the most advanced city and infrastructure. And yet foreigners complain about local skill sets?"

James was an ex-army man and marathon runner, and we walked at a brisk military pace. He was not against foreigner managers, but he believed the issues that I and others like me, were going through were mainly our fault. In many ways, he had a point. Foreign companies had rushed into these new markets; the new markets had not rushed into foreign companies. But what to do? Should those companies change their approach for locals, or should the locals change for the companies that hired them? The answer was found somewhere in between, but was either side listening?

James called foreign managers like me "gweilos," a Chinese term essentially meaning *ghost-man,* and it was an un-politically correct way to describe white Westerners. He was only sort of kidding when he called me this. There was a tension regarding cultures and race that organizations of all sizes were either ignoring or avoiding. But because the markets were doing well, the underlying issues were being ignored. James and I discussed the idea that foreign employees at Western companies were less likely to get promoted past certain levels of seniority. Was it because they didn't have the skills, or were cultural differences factoring in as to why some people got overlooked? James saw the United States especially as a place where people needed to be loud and self-promoting in order to advance. Coming from a part of the world where those same behaviors were shunned made promotion in these companies seem more daunting.

We debated; we argued. What seemed "loud" to James seemed to me like people speaking their mind and assertively going after the jobs they wanted. Who was right? Maybe we were both right.

I learned a lot during those walks, not only about different points of view but also about Singapore and how different it was than what I was used to. While it was a great place to do business, Singapore was known for its strict rules and regulations. It was illegal to sell chewing gum. Pornography of all kinds was banned. Films were censored, and the main newspaper was controlled by the state. Prostitution, however, was legal. You could walk down the street while drinking a beer. It was safe. Taxes were low and uncomplicated, taking five minutes to calculate and file. "Thank you for your contribution towards nation-building," said the friendly tax receipt. James and I discussed how this seemingly extreme government oversight stood in stark contrast to the laissez-faire business feel of the town. Where I saw a contradiction, he saw business as usual. Better yet, he saw coordinated efficiency.

Unwater your plants

Being so close to the equator, it was always hot. Really hot. More oppressive than the heat was the humidity. Singapore may be a city-state but, geographically speaking, it's a rainforest in a constant battle with cement. We walked through the city's parks, sometimes running for cover when the skies opened in world-ending monsoon, dodging the roots of a giant tree breaking through the sidewalk. In Singapore, it was not unusual to show up to a morning meeting half an hour late with the simple explanation of "it's raining," rendering tardiness completely understandable.

There's so much water vapor in the air, residents are required to unwater their plants. I learned this one day when a government inspector came to my apartment and politely asked if he could inspect the plants for excess water collecting at the bottom of pots. These pools of water evaporate so slowly they breed mosquitoes and mosquitoes can carry dengue. Dengue fever, also called "break bone fever," makes unwatering plants a very good idea.

During one walk with James, I was, as usual, saturated with sweat. James had nothing more than a barely perceptible glow—with his jacket on. He stopped and asked, "Hundred plus?"

My sunbaked brain translated. *He's asking me how I'm doing. If 100 percent means I'm doing well, 100 plus must mean he's asking if I'm doing great.* I decided my Singaporean English skills (known as Singlish) had advanced rapidly. I made an "okay" sign with my fingers and responded, "I'm a 110!"

It seemed I was getting the hang of things, having deftly overcome this mini-cultural communication moment. I was determined to win over locals like James. He nodded once and without noticeable expression headed toward a drink stand.

I was then handed an isotonic drink, similar to Gatorade. It was called "100 Plus."

He had been asking if I wanted a drink. 100 Plus drinks were as ubiquitous in the region as Coke. I felt like an idiot.

It started raining. A tropical downpour. We sipped our 100 Plus huddled together in a small gazebo seemingly designed for such an occasion.

Then my phone rang. It is was a client in California. "We need you to go to Cebu for a half a day a week."

"Cebu? Half a day a week?" I asked into the phone, not knowing what or where Cebu was. James, who couldn't help but hear my side of the conversation and who now knew I was clueless, mouthed "The Philippines."

The Philippines. Got it. I was scooping up any jobs that came my way, so I quickly agreed. While on the call, James looked at me concerned and poked my arm. "You know it's four plus away," holding up four fingers.

Four plus. Is this another drink? Thankfully, he elaborated. "Four-hour flight, at least."

I nodded a "thank you" and spoke into the phone. "You know, Cebu is a four-hour flight. Each way. That's a minimum of 8 hours of flying for 4 hours of work."

The client had no idea about the distances either. He paused, then said, "We can pay you to work for a full day each time. Your rates are cheaper than Jake, so it's not a problem."

There was not enough time to wonder what that meant.

"You can train large call center teams right?"

(Ghostbusters) "Yes."

"Great. Get to Cebu."

"Hey, maybe I should raise my rates if this guy charges so much more," I said, half-joking.

"You're *definitely* not Jake." The call ended.

Who is Jake, and what had I just agreed to?

The downpour stopped, and we resumed our walk. Work was flooding in. No sweat. I was clueless but feeling a hundred plus.

Those first few months of setting up a business overseas were a roller coaster. I kept getting tied up with many little mistakes, and often I didn't understand what was going on around me. At the same time, the growth of the region had lifted me and others forward, making it easy to discount or altogether ignore the challenges. As global growth accelerated, there were a lot of people faking their way through the expansion. The markets were hot, so many of us got away with it, but big challenges were lurking. Western companies wrestled with local hires and local companies wrestled with foreign hires. There was clearly something going on here, from miscommunication to different working styles. The global business landscape, while growing, seemed fractured when it came to the human side of business.

The upcoming trips to Cebu would expose me to these differences in more extreme ways, and I would finally begin to discover answers that would help me work through these people challenges.

Survival Guide Tips:

✔ To grow globally, get comfortable with being uncomfortable. Going global means facing new levels of uncertainty. *Sometimes you just have to go for it.*

✔ Be a localization detective. Invest time connecting with locals and encourage people to talk about their market knowledge and culture.

Chapter 3

Jake the Snake
and His Wonderful Cross-Cultural Data

"I'm now convinced that the worst thing a man can do with
a telephone without breaking the law is to call someone
he doesn't know and try to sell that person something he
doesn't want."

—*Michael Lewis*, Liar's Poker

When companies stick to their way of doing business, overseas expansion will faulter, or fail altogether. One company encountered these differences by moving its customer service center across the globe. How to overcome these differences? Cross-cultural research, going on for decades, can greatly help define and measure a lot of these differences in how people communicate and how business gets done.

T WAS 8 P.M. in Cebu, Philippines. Depending on daylight saving, Cebu is 12 hours ahead of the US East Coast. So while Americans were finishing breakfast, the sun was setting in Cebu and call center workers were about to start their night shift. They filed into the massive office building and began the daily ritual of waiting 11 minutes for an elevator to take them to their seats. So many American companies' call centers are based in Cebu that entire sections of the city operate on adjusted hours to enable the local workers to work and play according to the US time zones. Some bars in Cebu open at 6 a.m. and close at 1 p.m., with nightclubs staying open later.

As I drove into the office park compound, the car stopped at the first of many security checkpoints. The Philippines can be a rough place and these security stops were frequent. One guard opened and inspected the trunk and another circled the vehicle with a telescoping mirror to search for bombs underneath the car. Depending on the day, a bomb-sniffing dog might also be part of the security inspection. This was just the beginning. Before entering the building's lobby, I passed through several sets of metal detectors operated by gun-wielding security guards. And by guns, I mean large guns that mean business—the kind you usually only see in war movies. It seemed all for show—especially considering that all involved were just going through the motions, dulled by the routine. At times in the Manila airport, with a similar security setup, the metal detectors weren't even plugged in.

I got to the elevator lobby. It was remarkable how slow and inefficient they were. There was no coordination between these elevators; they were all going to the same floors, not communicating. It reminded me of dysfunctional teams where individuals were working hard, but poor management resulted in a massive waste of energy.

That being said, this inefficiency seemed to bother no one but me. The local workers were not annoyed by the insanely slow elevators. Time sensitivity did not exist here. And once inside the elevator, the chatter continued; some people sang. Some forgot to press the button to their floor.

If you find yourself in a place like this, missing the ordered efficiency of on-time elevators and frenetic businesspeople, just travel to Singapore for a taste of the familiar. The elevators in Singapore arrive quickly and efficiently, and once inside, no one speaks. The elevator has its job, as do the riders, and nothing will disrupt or delay this sense of purpose and order. The guy rapidly pushing the "close door" button as you try to get in…that's Singapore.

But we're not in Singapore anymore, Toto. I was in Cebu and had finally made it to my intended floor. Another useless metal detector? No, this one seemed more legitimate. And I was required to check my bag with the floor attendant. No personal items, including phones, were allowed on the main floor. And what the guards were most interested in keeping from the work area were USB flash drives. Health records, financial info, and more, these client lists were valuable and often quite easy to steal. All of this security was to prevent terrorists from getting in and client data from getting out. Three security checkpoints down and I finally met the team leader for the group of callers that I had been hired to train and coach. Her name was Jessie. She made $2.50 an hour, a respectable wage for the region.

Jessie was a bright-eyed 27-year-old with a surprising status symbol: she had a mouth full of shiny metal braces. That's right. Braces were a badge of honor for the rising socioeconomic class in cities like Cebu. Here, braces were sexy.

Jessie's commute was 90 minutes each way. She lived in a 800-square foot, three-room house with her family, along with her brother's wife and children. Tensions often ran high in small spaces, and Jessie's home was no exception. As in many families around the world, Jessie's mother didn't get along with Jessie's sister-in-law, which didn't help matters. There was no yard—no open space nearby. Children played on sidewalks beside street food vendors. Jessie lived in a religious home as well. Her family was Catholic with a post-missionary conversion twist—the family continued to worship their deceased ancestors and wore amulets to ward off evil spirits. Once, Jessie called in sick because her mother foresaw a tragedy in a dream and wouldn't allow her to go to work that day. Here in Cebu, mother knows best, even if it might cost you your job.

But right now, Jessie's shift was just beginning. After our introductions, the first thing she wanted to do was go downstairs and eat breakfast. The thought of dealing with the security checks and elevator delays merely to head downstairs for breakfast made me cringe. But this was Jessie's big chance to have a meeting outside the office, and I needed her on my side if I was going to turn around this project.

What seemed like ages later, we were back in the lobby. Jessie talked about her team's current calling campaign. There were half a million contacts in a database, all of whom had purchased a Hewlett Packard printer. Her team's objective was to call each contact from the database and sell a "service pack" for these printers. If a contact expressed an interest in this service pack, the individual was transferred to another agent to accept a form of payment. Jessie was unsure where these agents were geographically based.

"I heard this training was supposed to be done by Mr. Lowry," she said.

Who?

"Mr. Jake? Mr. Lowry? How do you say it?"

"Oh, Mr. Jake. Yeah, I'm replacing him."

"Do you train the same way as Mr. Jake? His ideas are not…normal. We prefer other normal ways," she said.

The man revered by his clients in the United States seemed to have quite a different reputation here in Cebu. Jessie leaned in and whispered, "We call him 'Jake the Snake' because no one likes him."

My curiosity about this man grew. *What* was he teaching these people that was not "normal"?

She went on to say, "He's running another program on the 12th floor. Hopefully you're better than him." She smiled and then looked at the food bill indicating my duty to pay.

While waiting for the elevator once again, I had a few moments to process this situation in Cebu. Jessie was great. She was personable, talkative, and self-confident, and even dressed in a way that reflected her outgoing personality, with bright colors and shiny jewelry. She presented herself in a way that was professional yet relatable. If her team was anything like Jessie, this initial session should be easy. I would meet and work with the team and then go find this Jake character.

Back upstairs in the office, I sat in an employee training room and read the call scripts, familiarizing myself with the tedious world that is ink jet printer service pack sales. Everything looked OK. My job was to figure out why the campaign was utterly failing.

Jessie and her teammates, many with braces-filled mouths, filed into the room. Only 21 of the 25 team members were present. Absenteeism was a daily problem, and these numbers were typical. Employee absences were routine and excuses were accepted with no questions asked. In a city as chaotic as Cebu, there could be legitimate reasons someone couldn't get into work. Traffic accidents turned roads into parking lots for hours at a time. People got sick because of mediocre sanitation. A strong family culture meant that if someone's parents decided something, it was done and that was final. And if traffic or illness or superstition didn't disrupt the workweek, the weather would. Changing weather patterns have made the Philippines even more of a magnet for tropical storms. Flooding brings entire cities to a standstill.

After quick introductions to those team members who made it to work that day, I was eager to get started. The team was dismissed to their stations and the cold calls began.

Sticking to the script

From a headset at Jessie's desk, I silently listened in to team members' phone calls. I connected to a random caller's line.

"Hello, Sir, is this a Mr. Tim-Othy Fred-REEK-son? Hello, Mr. Fred-REEK-son, my name is Banjo and I'm calling from HP, which stands for Hew-litt Pack-ard and we are a leading IT company. This call is regarding the HP printer you bought three years ago. Do you have a few minutes to talk? OK, great. As I said, Mr. Fred-REEK-son, you purchased this printer three years ago and the reason for my call today is to inform you that you have been selected for a special offer to purchase a service package entitling you to product support for this printer."

The response was quick but polite enough, "We no longer have that printer."

I looked down at the script provided for Banjo. Unfortunately, there was no option for this particular customer response. Since the caller did not know how to respond, he did the next best thing and stayed on script, "OK, that is good to hear. Sir, I would like to provide you with information on the benefits to this insurance plan including the additional two years of protection in case there is a problem with your printer." The man on the receiving end of the call was more polite than I expected. "I'm sorry, maybe it's a bad line, but I don't have the printer any longer, so I don't need insurance for it."

"Sir, I'd be happy to transfer you to an agent who can take your details so you can take advantage of this offer."

Click. The call was over.

It did not take a sales guru to identify the problem with this situation. What was disconcerting, however, was how this basic problem had gone unsolved despite happening repeatedly for more than a month. I looked at Jessie. She gave a look as if to say, "See? I told you so!" even though she hadn't mentioned this issue before.

Why hadn't the caller mentioned this problem to the floor manager? Why didn't the floor manager escalate this to her manager? Why didn't the problem then get mentioned to the client whose brand was being tarnished one call at a time?

The traditional business setup in the Philippines was hierarchal, maintaining a top-down approach. Managers disseminate information down the chain of command all the way to the callers in the cubicles. Rarely did information flow upward, no matter how valuable, from the caller to manager. While the assumption from Western business managers was that callers should provide feedback to managers, that's just not how it worked around here.

Why was this? If this same scenario had happened with a US-based call center team, this pertinent information would have quickly been identified, passed up the managerial chain, and reflected in a script change. However, 10,000 miles away, the reporting of feedback did not work in the same way. The callers didn't give Jessie the information about people throwing printers away rather than sending them for repairs. Even when Jessie discovered this problem, she didn't think she had the authority to raise the issue to senior managers, not to mention the fact that she found them difficult to communicate with. On top of everything else, she was too polite to cause trouble. Hierarchies like this die hard.

The script that Jessie and her team used did not include any options that matched the customer response. Without any other recourse, callers marked the response as a *non-interested customer* and simply moved on. Inaccurate data was captured and sent up the chain of command.

Why weren't these call centers operating the way they did in the United States, but for far less in labor costs? The call scripts hadn't changed. The targeted customers hadn't changed. But the people making the calls to those customers had changed. Geography and an understanding of cultural norms mattered when internally managing teams and when speaking with clients. Unfortunately, few companies had taken the time to figure this out, and in this industry it was not that surprising.

These "conversations" that callers have with customers are primarily and ultimately driven by cold hard metrics. The workers in the call centers weren't even discussed as human beings. Instead, they were counted as "seats": *This office has capacity for 2,000 seats. How many seats can we get for this price?* Across the call center industry, employees were referred to as furniture.

That worker who sits in a tiny cubicle stationed halfway across the world asking about your computer or healthcare or taxes as you're about to sit down to dinner isn't trying to annoy you. That worker is just following a script provided by their company.

This call center had managers reporting to people on the other side of the world who were not used to these working style differences. Without being on the ground to observe what was happening, easy-to-correct mistakes continued. Those security guards looking for USB sticks were searching for stolen customer data, but companies were ignoring the equally dangerous *bad* data being collected.

Callers were told to stick to the script, which they did, but at an embarrassing cost and clients kept hanging up.

I listened in to call after call. One little train wreck after another.

This kind of scenario happened frequently as businesses pushed projects globally without considering these unexpected impediments. In this case, invisible cultural differences had become the proverbial wrench in the machine, and that cost the company sales and hurt their brand.

Needing a moment to clear my head, I wandered away to find water. This was going to be a very long night. I turned a corner and bumped into a Westerner half my size and nearly knocked him to the floor. After apologies on both sides, he straightened his thick glasses, nodded politely, and hobbled off, disappearing into the farm of cubicles.

A caller who witnessed the accident said, "That was close. You almost killed Mr. Jake!" A few staff members nearby giggled.

The Snake.

Jake "the Snake" Lowry doesn't want me to write about him. The name Jake Lowry is fake. It's not Jake's lawyers I'm afraid of. It's how Jake himself goes after his enemies, mostly clients who are slow to pay invoices.

Jake had a 100% client payment rate.

His secret? Autodial software. Fail to pay and Jake would put your cell phone, home phone, and direct line at work in the autodial system of around 1,000 telemarketers. The software dials your number and the second you answer the phone, the call gets routed to an available telemarketer whose computer console provides any information included on the database.

Jake allegedly once put someone's name into 5,000 call center seats after an invoice was challenged. The guy changed all his numbers, thinking that would solve the problem. But the new number was procured and inserted into the systems.

I had found the legend. The tiny, now slightly injured, legend. Over several months I ended up spending a good deal of time with Jake, often at odd hours, having post-work drinks at 8 a.m. Day was night. Night was day. In Cebu, this was normal.

Jake's ability to get clients to pay was not the only phone-based psychological tactic he used. Born to an American father and Dutch mother, he grew up in the United States and graduated with a degree in psychology from a top university on the east coast. For a few years he managed a large call center based outside of Salt Lake City, Utah. Early in his career, Jake made his name by developing psychology-driven messaging for phone-based sales calls. He was a master at writing compelling scripts that had great success rates if the sales reps followed them, even if the product was terrible.

His secret was reverse psychology, saying the opposite of what a prospect expects. If the product was new, the caller says it really was not that new. If it was stronger than competitors, the sales rep says that other products might be as strong if not stronger. In fact, the purpose of many calls, according to Jake's scripts, was not to sell anything but simply to see how prospects were enjoying whatever competitive product they were currently using. This sales approach was to not sell anything, and it worked.

Without a sales pitch, prospects got lulled into a false sense of safety. Once the caller identified one gap, one area of weakness, unhappiness, or a point that could be a little bit better, he dropped one small selling point, subtly. *It sounds like that zoom-o-matic is great. It's easy to use and cleans up easily, even though from time to time it doesn't zoom everything, like carpets, it's really good. Our Boom-o-matic was made to deal with rugs, but I'll wrap this call up now because I don't want to take up any more of your time. Thank you so much for... what's that? How do WE deal with rugs? Well, maybe when you are ready to make a change, we can chat about that..."*

In the early 2000s, Jake's world began to change as more call center seats moved overseas. He watched as the office started shrinking and, before they laid off the last US-based caller in 2004, he had already left and set up his own consulting company. As more call center seats moved offshore, he spent most of his time living out of five-star hotels in places around the Philippines, India, Mexico, Bangladesh, Poland, and Malaysia. He had become an accidental business nomad. His business model had changed as well. Initially, he thought he would be helping enhance sales calls, but more and more he was being hired to help companies get these new offshore offices to work at all. Situations like the printer insurance issue I was working on were happening everywhere. Sure, the cost-savings were being achieved but customer satisfaction was plummeting.

Jake had identified two separate issues. First, Western headquarters assumed that people around the world worked in similar ways. For example, if an employee saw a problem, she'll speak up. While that may work in the United States, it wasn't working in the Philippines. This is what I was working through with Jessie and her team. A lot of these problems were easy to fix, but the trick was finding out there was a problem in the first place. The expectation was that if callers were told they can and should provide feedback up the food chain, they would do it. They thought flattening a hierarchy would be easy. Companies were starting to work in new countries but were sticking to their same old script.

The second challenge was the one Jake was more interested in solving. Psychology-driven training that worked so well for him in the United States was falling flat in other parts of the world. Why? It turned out that his trainings were great for Americans when they sold to other Americans. But the same approach wasn't working elsewhere. He began to research why callers were having trouble being successful over the phones.

Unfortunately, the rest of the call center industry was not as thoughtful as Jake. They panicked and made knee-jerk reactions, trying to fix problems before fully understanding the underlying issues.

The industry looked and listened to the differences they could see and hear, so they decided that *accents* were the problem. Since Indian callers were too "foreign" they needed to sound and act more like the people they were calling on the other side of the globe. They invested in classes to neutralize callers' accents. This didn't work. Sure, strong accents were a problem, but even people with softer accents were failing.

They made the callers sound more "American" by slapping western names like "Robert" over their real names. They tried technological tricks like getting caller IDs to show local numbers using area codes close to where the customer or prospect lived.

That did not work either. People on the end of the phone in English-speaking countries were annoyed and angry.

Then, in one of the more amusing moments in call center history, it was decided that in order to better connect with a Western audience, it was advisable to talk about local sports and weather.

Companies began investing in a kind of software that matched United States area codes with local news. This included local weather and sports scores that showed up on call center screens across India. "Robert" (whose real name was Hardik) would call a prospect in Chicago and, in his heavy Indian accent, awkwardly mention how cold it was and that the Bulls were doing well. This was the technological solution designed to overcome cultural differences.

The fad thankfully didn't last. It seemed people didn't appreciate being lied to, or at least being lied to poorly. Stories of "Robert" not realizing the Bulls were an NBA team were common. "Our Bulls are winning today, sir, are they not? They are very strong animals even in this cold weather, you know."

India as a call center haven quickly lost its allure. Companies began looking for another option, and they found it in the Philippines.

Filipino accents were more neutral, and people there had more ties to the West, especially the United States. Basketball was wildly popular. There were fewer Chicago Bulls mix-ups here. A big reason for this was that the United States has a long history of relations with the Philippines, the way the British did in India. Since 1898, the US has been closely connected, both good and bad, with the archipelago nation and continues to maintain a large military presence. A few thick fiber optic cables and economic development zones later, and the Philippines quickly became the call center capital of the world. Accents and sports. Problem solved.

Even with neutral accents and NBA knowledge, communication problems persisted. Conversations were ineffective. Beneath the accents were major cultural differences. Hierarchy and how it was expressed was one big example. In the Philippines, a caller wouldn't point out a problem with a script because it wasn't how things were done. It was ironic that crystal-clear phone systems could connect humans in any part of the world, but the technology did nothing for helping humans to actually *connect*.

And this was why our paths awkwardly collided in Cebu. Jake was here trying to get a local team to effectively handle sales conversations all over the world. And he thought he had cracked the code.

Measuring working styles across the planet

Jake had uncovered a data-driven approach that could be used when communicating across cultures.

People don't buy things in the same way. They do not want customer support the same way. They do not communicate in the same way. His answer was to adapt each conversation based on this cross-cultural data.

We became fast friends mainly because I was one of the few people who wanted to hear about how he found, and used, his data sets. Over several trips, we got together after work and dug into the details.

"I was trying to figure out how to get callers to communicate better with Americans, so I wrote scripts that sounded more 'American.' I made the message more direct, more informal and respectful of time. But what happens when the next call is to someone in Mexico, Peru, India or Estonia? How does a caller figure out the right communication for each conversation?" Jake listened to thousands of calls from different countries and took notes. Americans were polite but impatient, while the Brits were also polite but more patient. Sarcasm from the UK was going over everyone's head in Cebu, and if a caller missed this, it immediately put the prospect off. Saudis expected to be spoken to formally and seemed quick to hang up if upset. French went off topic before making decisions. Indians seemed to talk a lot and say yes, but they would not do what they had just agreed to do. Malaysians hardly talked at all. Brazilians spoke loudly and shouted regardless of whether they were happy or angry. Jake's findings bothered him because he felt like he was staring at a list of cultural stereotypes. Was any of this valid or helpful?

He was collecting anecdotes but needed evidence.

Was there any data that backed up what the team was experiencing over the phones? His curiosity was rewarded when he uncovered decades of research focusing on specific ways cultures vary in work situations. This turned out to be a goldmine for anyone willing to dig through the stuff.

Jake was normally a quiet guy, but when he started talking about data he got unusually animated. We were having dinner at a café in the lobby of a hotel in Cebu. I was distracted by the large metal detector inside the front door. A sizeable amount of people were declaring their handguns hidden under their clothing. Jake as usual was talking about his cross-cultural data.

He noticed I was preoccupied by the weapons and said, "You see how those guns are hidden inside that guy's shirt? That's the culture bit I'm talking about, the things that are hidden from plain sight but really important. All of these managers trying to build customer-facing teams worry about accents and local sports—things they can see and hear—but it's the invisible things that really matter."

He was talking about differences in how people approach work in different parts of the world. This included how a person perceives time, how they handle relationships, how they approach difficult conversations, and how they build trust. These working styles were, as Jake said, invisible, but once understood went a long way in understanding what made people around the world tick.

"Researchers have studied how people across the world perceive time. The answer varies considerably. Some places are time sensitive while others are much more flexible about when things get done," he told me as one example. This was easy to observe. The Philippines was not time sensitive, from the slow elevators to the fact that we sat down for dinner 45 minutes earlier and hadn't even been given menus. Jake used these findings regarding time and changed the first sentence of his call scripts. Germany and the United States were extremely time sensitive. "In these countries you ask for only a few *seconds* of someone's time. In places less concerned with time, you ask for a few *moments* or don't mention time at all."

Jake used two primary sources of research: the GLOBE Project[1] and Geert Hofstede.[2] Through massive surveys, both studies look at how cultures affect organizations and businesses. Both have published their findings, laying out these style differences around the world. In terms of seeking evidence, he had hit the cross-cultural jackpot.

In another example, data showed the variation of how hierarchies—how people respond to power—vary across the globe. Power mattered everywhere, but how it mattered and how much it mattered varied considerably. Countries with higher focus on hierarchies, sometimes called *power distance*, tend to prefer higher levels of formality, especially when a caller is speaking to someone more senior. In some parts of the world, a speaker must first figure out the status of the person with whom they are speaking because the words change depending on the answer.

*   *   *

People expect to be addressed by their last names in a place like Russia and Saudi Arabia because these are places with a high degree of power distance. As the adage goes, *the customer is always right*, but in high power distance countries, the customer is even more right, so in these cases, callers needed to be more deferential. The Philippines was also a high power distance country and Western companies accustomed to a lower power distance work setting were getting tripped up by this invisible difference. People from countries with less of a focus on hierarchies tended to speak up to senior managers. They also tend to prefer more informal language. Callers could use first names and could be more opinionated. New Zealand, Australia, and the Scandinavian countries all stand out as low power distance countries.

Dealing with yes and no around the world

"Do you know the two most dangerous words in the English language?" I stopped watching a man removing a giant Colt 45 out from under his shirt and focused on Jake. He continued, "They are *yes* and *no*. They are confusing and cause all sorts of issues." The word *yes* can mean many things based on context.

Do you understand? *Yes* is a common response, even if the truth is *no*.

Jake had a point. There were so many examples where these little words caused big issues in work settings.

Is this project going to be completed on time?

Do these instructions make sense?

Would you like to buy this product?

Often, the answer that came back was yes, regardless of the real answer.

Jake researched this phenomenon as well. The data showed trends around the world of where yes meant *yes*, where it meant *maybe,* or where it meant *no.* Social psychologists had been looking at this trait for decades, and now people like me and Jake were applying it to international teams.

Data on communication styles suggest that there are cultures that have *direct* communication styles, which means people communicate…directly. They say what they mean. Truly direct communication means that the receiver of the message does not have to read between the lines. The Netherlands, the United States, and Germany all score as direct communicating cultures. Compare that to *indirect* communication, which is more nuanced. Indirect communicators may say what they have to say in their own way and let the reader interpret the rest. Indirect communication often relies on tone and body language to help convey the speaker's point. The phrase "that's not too bad" actually means *that's good*, and is a favorite with United Kingdom natives. However, this causes confusion outside of the British Isles when people who don't understand the phrase think they are doing something wrong.[3] If it is not bad, then what is it? To add to the confusion, the phrase, "that's pretty good," can mean it is *not* good. It depends on the tone or inflection. If the receiver does not know how to interpret this kind of tone, the key message can be lost entirely. A British friend of mine once described how a taxi driver ripped her off by taking a longer route. She said, "I was so upset, *I almost said something.*" That's indirect communication. Ironically, compared to a majority of the people on the planet, the UK is considered a direct communicating culture.

Indirect communication works perfectly fine if both people are in sync with the communication style, but quickly causes confusion when one speaker is accustomed to speaking one way and the other person is more familiar with to communicating another way.

Countries that score as high indirect communicators include France, Saudi Arabia, India, Thailand and, most of all, Japan. In many parts of the world, for example, it was considered impolite or rude to say no. It was simply not how things were done. Direct communicators working in these kinds of cultures kept hitting roadblocks because they asked closed-ended questions—questions that anticipated either a *yes* or a *no.*

In Jake's typical binary way he said, "If someone has been conditioned never to say no, then why would you ask that person a yes-or-no question? You will only get one answer."

The data sets defined these different working styles and ranked countries based on the results of the research. Jake took all of these rankings on how places perceive time, how they consider hierarchies and their communication styles, and he built a software program.

He replaced the sports and weather updates with messaging that adjusted to local cultural norms. Calling into the United States created a different script than Mexico. The UK differed from France. India sounded totally different from Russia. He had dozens of variations, all automatically written based on the culture data.

Here is an example of how it worked.

One of Jessie's teammates called a person in Mumbai, India, who bought a printer two years ago. "*Mr. Reddy* (India has a high power distance, therefore use the more formal last name). *You bought a printer from HP around two years ago and I wanted to see if I could take a few minutes* (flexible time) *to see how it is working out for you?* (Indirect communication style = open-ended questions and avoiding yes/no questions.)

To correct for this possibility of a *yes* that really meant *no*, Jake's scripts avoided close-ended questions when working in indirect communicating parts of the world. When his callers were asked to confirm a sale or schedule another appointment, they would say, "I wonder if we were to move this forward with another call, what day next week would work best for you?"

For direct communicating cultures such as the United States, Germany, and Australia, the messaging would change to "would you like to move forward with this?" A close-ended question in this case had a higher likelihood of working.

These adjustments helped the callers and their success rates improved. More important, these data can help anyone better understand and react to overseas situations, and it does not require software. It takes a willingness to learn about the different working styles across the planet and to practice changing communication styles accordingly. Of course data won't solve all the problems, but it was a big step in the right direction. (Links to the data sets can be found in this chapter's endnotes.)

Seeing the day-in-the-life of Jessie and her team of callers in the Philippines confirmed why moving services-based jobs around the world was harder than companies expected.

As for Jake, his cold personality did him little favors. Even though his approach was ahead of its time, he was unable to grow his business because he was terrible at building relationships. Jake could sell anything, except himself. These days Jake is reportedly working away at next-generation robo-calling technology, determined to take the *humans* out of the sales process entirely.

Survival Guide Tips:

✔ To communicate effectively, use data to understand the invisible cultural differences that lead to miscommunication. Clear communication technology does not equal clear communication.

✔ Your natural working style is probably not wrong, but in overseas markets it is probably not right. Take the time to understand different working styles and learn to adapt.

Chapter 4

The Centurions and
Mr. Asshole's lunch
secret

"Every experience, no matter how bad it seems, holds within it a
blessing of some kind. The goal is to find it."

—Anonymous

Expatriates, even those who misbehave, provide each other
with tips and guidance to working overseas. How to lead
diverse teams? How to manage up? How not to bribe border
patrol? The millions of new global workers don't have this
insider knowledge, so the following story will help.

THE NAKED, barefoot man walked up the fairway of the 18th hole. The equatorial sun did his pasty British birthday suit little favors. Cradling a golf club and a beer in one hand, he doffed his hat with the other and tipped it in our direction in gentlemanly fashion. I was on a patio overlooking the golf course with a group of his friends. We heckled and applauded as he made his way leisurely up the perfectly manicured course to finish his round.

An Indonesian couple practicing on the nearby putting green, both wearing impeccable golf attire, stopped and starred. Shocked, the woman let a putter slide from her hand.

Meet the *Centurions*. Named because none of the founders of the informal club can get a ball around a golf course in under one hundred shots—an abysmal record. This expatriate group with members in Singapore and Hong Kong has carried on the centuries-long tradition of people behaving badly overseas. Monthly get-togethers included an awful lot of drinking, occasional golf games and chaos. There was always chaos.

In some ways their antics reminded me of the many foreign companies who venture overseas—disregarding local customs and behaving like they have a free pass to do whatever they wanted because headquarters thousands of miles away could not—or did not want to—see what they were up to.

What could be learned about working globally from the Centurions? Quite a lot. Their years of living as expats had formed a treasure trove of lessons about working effectively with overseas teams. Maybe all that time abroad had also dulled some of their social senses, which was why they could be found terrorizing golf courses around the region. The strange thing was that the biggest lesson I took from this group was on the topic of team trust and how it was earned. Sure, they were troublemakers, but when work situations got tough, many of these guys were dependable, which could not be said about many other foreign managers who looked at the region more as a stepping-stone to better things rather than a place to win hearts and minds.

If Jake from Cebu was a black-and-white walking dataset, here were colorful characters, whose faults in some cases seemed to help make them effective working in unpredictable markets. These guys were tough and resilient when it came to getting things done in complex work situations. These lessons were not always pretty, which brings me back to our naked golfer.

His name was Roger Staddon and he was one of the top regional managers for a software company that helped other online companies handle customer support issues. Rather than pay a call center like mine to handle customer questions, his company sold a system that enabled customers to communicate with each other and help answer their own questions. On weekends, he was a Centurion.

Most of his local staff loved the guy. When senior managers from his company's UK headquarters came through town, Roger single-handedly convinced the team not to quit because of how patronized they felt from the visiting leadership. He spent a lot of time with his teammates, and they knew he had their backs. One proof point came when one of his employees mistakenly sent a confidential internal email to a client who complained about it to Roger's boss. It would have been easy to blame the employee who made the mistake, but instead Roger defended him, arguing the mistake caused no damage and how the employee had learned a lesson in accountability. Roger's skill in storytelling managed to keep the UK team content. His team saw this kind of protection and rewarded him with their loyalty.

Calibrated storytelling

How did he manage up so well? Roger understood that his company's headquarters didn't know what was happening on the ground across regions. They never did. Other managers got this messaging wrong, either giving their headquarters too much or not enough information.

Either way, executives would get suspicious and start micromanaging ineffectively from a distance. Roger had found the right mix of delivering enough information without overdoing it. Specifically, when updating his boss back at headquarters, his approach was to start with a small story highlighting whatever point he was making, then include relevant data, then explain why his boss needed to know (he was either helping her make money or save money), then he'd wrap up with another story driving at his point.

Let's say he had to present to senior managers back in the UK about pricing issues across APAC—a common challenge for many companies. Roger would start with a mini story, something like "Our largest competitor has just changed their pricing model in India, and it's worth us looking at why they did this." Next, he would share the data. "You can see how this maps closely with the price sensitivity studies we've looked at in the past. We also have data showing how we may quickly lose market share if we don't make a similar adjustment." He would then add another small story about another company in different industry who had found themselves in a similar situation and a positive lesson that was learned.

The point was this: the guy did his homework and then expertly communicated his findings and recommendations to headquarters. While this may sound like common sense, it was becoming clear that when working globally, common sense was the exception rather than the rule. There were countless calls between local leaders and their overseas bosses where the message was poorly thought through and delivered. Comments like, "We're too expensive here and need to lower our prices," may be correct, but did nothing to win over headquarters. Roger's storytelling was *calibrated*, and he knew how to prepare and deliver his messages. This was how he managed his managers so well. Headquarters rewarded him by leaving his team alone, which everyone appreciated. One of his competitors, a larger, well-known company, spent years churning through regional directors because the directors kept giving headquarters either too much or too little information. The perception was that there was either too much complaining or too much hiding. Roger produced similar results but had lasted for half a dozen years running the region. He was able to hang on simply because he knew how to tell a better story to the higher-ups while maintaining a strong level of trust with his people on the ground.

One day each month Centurions would leave Singapore and head to either Malaysia or Indonesia, where prices for everything were cheaper and the rules, while technically stricter, were not frequently enforced. The alcohol consumption was difficult to comprehend. They would meet at a ferry terminal at 7 a.m. where cans of Tiger beer—the first of many—were passed around. That wasn't the astonishing part. Many of the guys had been out the night before until 4 a.m. or later. Twelve beers per person during the round of golf was average. And this was at the equator, where the temperature in the early morning starts off at 90 degrees Fahrenheit and goes up from there. And that doesn't include the humidity.

Drinking continued after the morning game, throughout the post-round meal, and during the commute across borders. A bus would take them directly back to the local bar, where the session burned through the night. Annual "tours" involve this lifestyle for three days straight. Some stay on for an "extended tour," lasting up to five days. Hotels got wrecked and there were frequent bar fights.

Every time I took a ferry over to Indonesia or Malaysia with the Centurions, it felt like I was stepping onto the *Nellie*, the boat from *Heart of Darkness*. I wanted to learn from these guys, but this was a dangerous ride. There was something addictive about being surrounded by many people who didn't care about basic social decency. The scariest thing would be for these outings to be considered normal. I sometimes felt guilty for even being nearby. Was I an accomplice? You bet. Charlie, who was a partner at a large international law firm, assured me of that. "As your lawyer, I advise you to look the other way right about now."

Most incidents could be sorted out with a little bit of cash, and this happened frequently due to loud, drunken antics. I should have run the other way, but I didn't. While they were above-average jerks when they got together, they were above-average businessmen when it came to managing emerging markets.

Total accountability

Smitty, my grizzled friend from chapter 1, was a Centurion and often the first to throw a punch in a bar if he felt the situation warranted it. He also had loyal employees who trusted him. They liked him for the simple reason that he got things done. He was "a doer." In November 2008, when Mumbai experienced the first in a series of terrorist attacks that resulted in more than 150 deaths, Smitty was immediately on the phone making sure his team members in the area were safe and helped to arrange transport out of the city. Granted, he did it from a bar, but his quick response was more effective than most companies who spent ages in "emergency response" meetings trying to get a consensus for what to do next. Two days after the event, he received instructions from his UK headquarters as to how he should respond, including approval for his Mumbai team to spend extra money, if necessary, to leave the city. These late, board-approved instructions were useless. Smitty had solved the problem in real time. Employees across the region knew he was the person to turn to if they wanted to ensure something got done.

VUCA knows VUCA

One note I scribbled on a soiled bar napkin at a Centurion event read: *VUCA knows VUCA.*

Volatility, Uncertainty, Complexity and *Ambiguity.* A military acronym for decades, VUCA, had become a trendy term in the business community, and for good reason. It summed up modern working conditions quite well. The Centurions knew how to handle

VUCA moments. Think what you want of these guys, when something at work blew up, these were the people you wanted on your side.

Maybe it paid to be a little volatile, uncertain, complex, and ambiguous if that was the kind of environment you work in. Thankfully, I met a Centurion named Axel. Better behaved than the rest of this group, he was a character who thrived in a VUCA world but didn't need to terrorize everyone in his path. He acted as my blast shield, protecting me from the likes of naked Roger and fighting Smitty, and he helped unearth little diamonds of business advice hidden within the mounds of Centurion dirt.

Axel was safe. He was reliable and steady. Originally from the Netherlands, he was a serial expat with more than 20 years of experience living in rough parts of the world: Nigeria, Siberia, Houston. Axel was never afraid to uproot his wife and kids. He worked for energy companies and, more recently, a large industrial outfit headquartered in Europe that sent him on assignments around the world. He was a bad golfer with no natural coordination, but he kept at it. He was also incredibly direct,[1] pointing out that I acted like an uptight, prudish American.

During golf, he lectured me as we slashed our way through jungle growth searching for his ball. There was an unspoken agreement that I would help him find his golf game and he would help me find my way.

"Everything about you screams 'American,'" he said in his Dutch accent. "Your clothes are too big. Your smile is too big, your...nonsmile is too big, and you point out obvious things like, 'Hey, this food is so spicy but still so good.' You need to shut up more." I took his comments in stride and tried not to smile or nonsmile too much. He really did mean well.

"It's funny that I spend so much time in Asia, especially given my name," he once told me as we drove around the course, avoiding drunken, half-clothed Centurions.

"Chinese cultures put your last name first and your first name last. It's because family is so important right? That's why they'll call you Mr. whatever your name is. Me? I'm 'Mr. Axel.'"

"OK, but why is that funny?"

"The problem is that the letter 'X' is pronounced like a 'sh' and when you add the accents…"

I made the connection. "You're Mr. Asshole!"

"Ya."

Axel checked into hotels and watched the poor clerk stutter and hesitate before saying, "Your room is ready, Mr.…. Asshole."

Not skinny. Not fat. His hair was a bit longer than short, not blond, but not dark. He quickly became my go-to mentor. He'd have a war story relevant to any work problem I brought his way. A decade later I credit much of what I have learned about doing business overseas to his crude, but wise, advice.

It's not what you say, it's how you are perceived

Axel managed to point out my faults and stupidity in the middle of every story. He'd give an example and insert me into it, as if I was the one who had committed whatever heinous cultural gaffe he was explaining. By the end, he'd end up replacing the character with me.

"There was an Australian guy who took over a team across Asia. The dumbass tried to give a speech to his team to motivate them. He actually told the locals who reported to him that *they didn't work for him, but that he worked for them.* He was trying to be their buddy, ya?"

"He wanted to be the humble but inspiring leader, saying everyone is in this together as equals. He talked about how he was here to help them succeed, and that they were the experts in their country, and he needed their help to work together. That kind of crap. It sounds like something stupid you would do."

I always took the bait. "What's wrong with what he said?"

"You can't say that stuff in this region. Hierarchies in teams are different in different countries and need to be treated differently. Why would you say that? You just told your whole team you didn't know what you were doing and they can't rely on you to lead! You fool!"

"But it wasn't me. I—"

"It doesn't matter what you think you are saying. It's what people *hear.*"

He was talking about the importance of adapting to situations, and I was willing to take any and all insults in order to learn from him. By Axel's logic, what you say isn't important, it's how you are perceived. Maybe he wasn't intending to insult me, but that's how I was interpreting it.

"Teams in different parts of the world need different kinds of leaders. Sometimes you need to lead people in a top-down way even though it may not be what you're used to."

In his own, politically incorrect way, Axel was yelling an important lesson. Leading people required different approaches depending on where you were. Jack Welch's idea of leading with your gut might not always work in foreign markets because if your gut guides you based on experiences and surroundings, how is it supposed to work in new environments? The desire to have everyone on a team work as equals will fail if some of those people have been programmed all their lives to believe that they are not equal.

Hierarchy matters everywhere, but it is more important in some parts of the world than others. In the call center, Jake had pointed this out and it also turned out to be an obsession of Axel's. So many business mistakes were made because of misunderstandings around hierarchies.

Axel made his point with examples. He once had an idea to make a slight design change to his company's product. He thought the adjustment might solve problems for clients and increase their sales. With teammates reporting to him from several countries, what was the best way for him to get feedback for this new idea?

In Australia, a low power distance country, hierarchy was not that important. He told his Australian teammates the idea and asked for feedback. Pretty straightforward. But how did he get feedback from teammates who came from places with stronger hierarchies? A straightforward approach would not get the honest feedback he wanted.

His other teammate was in Indonesia, a high power distance country. If asked, this teammate's opinion would be more likely to agree with the new product change regardless of what he really thought. Why? Because Axel was the boss and what the boss says goes. It's not normal to question the boss, even if the boss's idea was terrible. This was hierarchy in action. Therefore, to get real feedback, a different approach was needed.

"In a place like Indonesia, I asked for the teammates to put together their ideas on the subject *before* even mentioning my idea. I told the team that *some clients might be interested in solving this extra problem using our existing product. Could you send me some ideas as to how this might get done?*"

He had adjusted to treat people the way *they* wanted to be treated. It worked, too. By adapting, he was able to collect ideas and develop new versions of products that would never have come out of a boardroom thousands of miles away. This was how global innovation was supposed to work. From there he made sure everyone on his team shared the recognition.

Conflicting realities

The data that Jake had on cross-cultural studies was a good start, but here were real examples showing how the data could be used. In this case, Axel was adjusting his approach based on how people respond to hierarchies. This was how he adapted to *power distance.* I started thinking about my own team and the issues I was having with my project manager. Was there an invisible hierarchy I wasn't handling correctly? Axel would explain these bits of wisdom as we commuted to our weekend getaways. The lessons weren't always theoretical, they were experiential as well. One time while standing in line for passport control with Roger nursing a morning beer, the two of them showed me how to bribe border guards.

Why would we want to do this? To avoid filling up our passports with stamps too quickly. Passport pages were precious and took time and money to replace.

"Consider today's destination, Indonesia," Axel said, after making eye contact with a border patrol guard standing at one end of the passport control. He slid a $10 Singapore bill into each of our passports. "Bugger this queue. Follow me." Ten dollars was the going rate to keep a page unstamped and to avoid the long lines.[2] "These guys working here don't care. Do you know what they get paid? Pretty much nothing. Everyone up the chain gets paid very little, officially. This is why they are open to workarounds."

"You mean corruption."

He sighed, handing over the passports. The guard eyed Roger's drink with disdain. We waited for only a moment before being led to a side door and quickly escorted through an office to the arrivals hall. *Corruption* was a tricky word when it came to doing business around the planet.

"They don't consider it that. In a place that's broken, you can pay to get things fixed. It works very well." He pointed to a clean page on his passport and waved at the fact we were through immigration faster than anyone else.

"Sounds like mafia stuff to me."

"Now you're getting it. Hey, by the way. You want to try to pay off a guard in Singapore?"

"Um, no way."

"Yes, NO WAY. Because their systems work. The top government people get paid millions of dollars as their salary. It's crazy to us, but it works. No 'corruption.'"

A few years earlier, Ben Karber, another Centurion and one of the few Americans in the group, nearly lost his job when he got caught up in a situation involving something that *seemed* like corruption to his company in the United States, but to locals was nothing of the sort. He learned the expensive way that corruption was in the eye of the beholder.

Ben was settling into his general manager role for APAC when he interviewed a Singaporean for a position focused on selling to the Singapore government. The applicant had little to no relevant experience and came to the interview without a résumé. Instead, he pulled out his wedding photo album. As far as the candidate was concerned, he did not need to understand the product. He was there to point out all the important government leaders who were his guests. In squeaky-clean Singapore, like everywhere else, who you knew mattered.

Ben decided not to hire the guy because the whole thing seemed against the company policy. His United States headquarters would flip out if they knew someone was being hired based on their wedding guest list. The candidate was told this was not how their company operated. But this decision turned into an unexpected catastrophe. Word quickly spread on the street that the company was not serious about selling to the public sector. No salesperson with government experience would touch them. What should have been a multimillion-dollar-a-year revenue stream turned to nothing and stayed that way for half a decade.

He was dealing with two conflicting realities. On one hand were the rules of his company and ethical hiring practices. On the other hand, there were the local realities where relationships sometimes trump skills. These two worlds did not overlap, but it was Ben's job to make them coexist. Maybe he should have hired the guy and kept quiet about the photo album, or maybe he should have looked elsewhere but come up with some face-saving reason for not hiring the candidate. Instead, he handled it in a black-and-white manner, by being direct. It nearly cost him his job, and it cost the company millions of dollars in lost business.

"You'll get there," Axel reassured me. Mr. Axel was the first person I really got to know who had a global mindset. The modern nomadic lifestyle fit him just fine. He took a globally flexible approach toward life and spoke a lot about *values* and how different they can be across the globe. Not only did he enjoy this topic, he thrived on it. "Values are a funny thing because they are these simple ideas that people take seriously but rarely live up to. Then people get pissed off when someone else's values differ from their own. I mean, who cares? No one is living up to them anyway! Why don't people just go with the flow?"

Axel could hold two conflicting opinions in his mind and have no qualms about it. His world was one of ambiguity, and he was naturally comfortable with it in his own way.

A conversation could begin on the topic of the Dutch government considering censorship of websites—a position he vehemently opposed—and then turn to China's censorship laws, where he would question anyone who pushed back on China's right to control all data coming into and out of the country. You were an idiot if you thought China would change their approach. And you were an idiot if you believed what China said at face value. It was the fault of companies and other governments that kept failing in China, because they should have known the Chinese do things their own way. Axel did not see contradictions; he saw truths that held wildly different characteristics and was somehow comforted by this variation.

Having lived in over half a dozen countries and worked in countless others, he didn't really think of himself as a citizen of anywhere. He said he was from the Netherlands, but he didn't seem to be particularly emotionally connected to it. At Axel's apartment in Singapore, we would "watch" his kids, which meant that we'd sit somewhere drinking in the condo complex while his 3- and 5-year-old boys did whatever they wanted, wherever they wanted to do it.

"I am Dutch but the Netherlands (he pronounced it "Nederlands") is not my home. My home is here," he'd say pointing to his kids, on the rare occasion they were in sight. "*And now my home is dere,*" his finger followed the children as they zigged and zagged around a playground, dangling dangerously off a raised balance beam. Another parent came running over to help before they toppled over. Ironically, Axel didn't abandon all of his native traditions. He and his wife were proudly raising their kids in what they called the "Dutch way," which focused on independence and self-reliance. This parenting style seemed to clash with the other parents in their condo complex, as evidenced by the dirty looks thrown in our direction.

Home was his latest posting. "When I am with a Singaporean, I am Singaporean. When I'm with an American asshole," pointing to me, "I am an American asshole as well. You," he paused choosing his next word carefully, "have to *adjust* as needed." Axel knew he could insult me because I didn't mind. To others he would behave completely differently.

He stared at a caterpillar inching along our table. At certain times throughout the year this type of caterpillar appeared en masse and just as quickly vanished. "We can learn from these guys. They know how to change throughout their life, eh?"

Axel was a master of change. In fact, his most impressive skill was his ability to adapt to different situations.

The lunch secret

With his team in Singapore, Kuala Lumpur or Hong Kong, his policy was to eat lunch twice a day. As odd as it sounded, this was the bedrock of his management approach. "You always should have lunch with some, or all, of your team," he declared. Eating at noon with a group, he'd come back to the office and turn right around and head out with the 1 p.m. lunch crowd.

"I bet you don't like eating lunch with people during workdays. You think it's a waste of time?" He didn't give me a chance to agree and instead plowed forward with his lecture. "This is one of the core reasons Americans piss the rest of the world off, because you are so focused on getting from point A to point B, you look at food as merely a pitstop, a moment to refuel, so you can keep rushing to get the job done."

"What's wrong with being focused on results?"

Axel finished his gin in a gulp with his eyes bulging at my naivete.

"You ignore the importance of relationships, but you don't real-ize that it is relationships that drive results." I thought about this. He smiled at me and muttered "Americans!" as he refilled his glass.

Lunch in many Asian countries was the third rail of the business day. It was not to be messed with. A 60- to 90-minute lunch break was considered standard, and executives visiting from places like the United States, who often came over because an office was under-performing, would deliver a "we need to double our efforts" kind of speech only to find everyone disappear to the food courts for what seemed like half the work day. By 5 or 6 p.m., the executive would take the team out for drinks to continue discussions and do a for-eign version of relationship building. But in some parts of the world, employees don't want to catch up after work for drinks. If they did get dragged out, they often sneak out of the bar and head back to work. So, while the Western boss was out having drinks and complaining about the long lunch breaks, the local team was back in the office working. It was a common, and classic, case of misunderstanding.

"Have you ever worked out of London? Try telling a team they can't head to the pub after work because they must stay later. See how effective that is. Messing with lunchtime in Asia is the same thing."

Axel had dozens of pictures of noodles on his phone. "People here love their food. You don't get it," he'd say pointing an accusing finger my way. "They take photos of everything they eat. They post them online." He showed me a picture of a bowl of noodles. He was right. I didn't get it. I hadn't had lunch with my project manager, Jing Yi, even once. In fact, I'd ask her to bring lunch back to the office if we needed to work through a client issue.

"Lunchtime is sacred. Never mess with it. You Americans eat at your desk or eat by yourself. When I am in America, that's what I do, too."

Once, as I was heading to an appointment downtown, I stumbled across one of these multi-lunch sessions. It was impressive. Sitting at an indoor food center was Axel and five of his Singaporean colleagues. I watched from a distance as they chatted away in between slurping down bowls of noodles. It was as if he'd been transformed. Even though I couldn't hear them, it was obvious there was none of Axel's usual biting insults and sharp, lectures. His body language had changed. He looked smaller and unimposing. Relaxed and totally engaged in whatever it was they were talking about.

For almost 15 minutes I stood there watching these people eat lunch, nearly missing my meeting.

It was his state of mind that made Axel so successful at working with teams across the globe. His attitude gave him patience, which made people comfortable and prevented issues from festering. I was learning that this skill—patience—was one of the most important pieces to figuring out how to crack the puzzle of managing international teams. It was Mr. Asshole's lunch secret. And it was why his teams performed so well. By slowing down, he managed to speed up results.

The boom in companies expanding into emerging markets meant that countless expat managers came through on assignments ranging from weeks to years. They'd all make the same mistakes over and over like I had done, pushing for quick progress and not understanding that there were multiple ways to get things done.

Over several years I brought some of my toughest work problems to Axel. Often while we sat in a golf cart (which is called a buggy pretty much everywhere outside the United States), waiting out a tropical downpour or man-made Centurion delay, such as an overturned buggy or a man in a pond.

"When you walk into my sales team's office, you can hear a pin drop," I told him. "You'd think you were in the finance department." I had heard this line from countless company heads who were having the same problem. No one ever seemed to be on the phone. "How can you sell stuff if you don't talk with people?"

"Esses and Sees," he replied. "Dat's your problem."

I sighed. Was that a Dutch expression I should somehow know?

He wasn't going to elaborate. We played on. At the end of the round, as I stumbled out of the buggy, Axel walked over to me, looking alert and sober and said three words:

"Check out DISC."

Axel understood better than most how people operated and he knew how to adjust accordingly. His advice was about to take me down the road of behavioral profiling, and his cryptic "esses and sees" diagnosis will be explained in the next chapter. He, along with Roger the storyteller, and Smitty the doer all managed to build trust within their teams and used different ways to do it. In fast-moving, international settings, trust was hard to create and maintain, but they made it happen. Roger defended his local team, even when they messed up, and he used stories to persuade his headquarters to let him run the region his way, while Smitty was in his element during emergencies, neither hesitating nor getting caught up in corporate politics. The three of them were masters at working in VUCA environments, even if it meant letting out a little bit of VUCA on the weekends.

Survival Guide Tips:

✔ To improve communication, use *calibrated storytelling*. Persuasion happens when strong data meets a good story, so do your research and deliver regular updates through helpful anecdotes.

✔ To avoid misunderstandings, remember it's not what you say, it's how you are *perceived*. Always confirm your message is clear by asking follow-up questions.

Chapter 5

Breaking the
Golden Rule

" 'Who in the world am I?' Ah, that's the great puzzle!"

—Alice's Adventures in Wonderland

"Treat people the way you want to be treated." Nope. Working globally means breaking some rules. Let's start with this golden one and replace it. "Treat people the way *they* want to be treated." To do this well, team leaders must first know themselves and those they work with. How? Behavioral profiling is a great starting point.

AXEL POINTED his finger at me, "Who—are—YOU?" This was an especially good question considering our surroundings, because at that moment we were sitting in the Loi Kroh bar complex in Chiang Mai, a city in the north of Thailand. We were on a Centurion's tour weekend and, of course, had found ourselves sitting in a seedy bar watching a Muay Thai boxing match. A tattooed dwarf was fighting a man twice his size while bar girls targeted clusters of pale, overweight tourists. Each day of boozy golf in the sun ended at some shady bar like this one and, oddly enough, it was the perfect location for deep introspection.

Axel, as always, seemed right at home and continued talking. "If you don't really know who *you* are, the rest is pointless. You can't lead people from different parts of the world until you know yourself first. Strengths and weaknesses. What gives you your energy, what aggravates you, and so on. First, think about YOU." He reached for the icy bucket of Singha beers.

In many ways, working with people from different parts of the world and, often remotely, was the new business management challenge. Leadership gurus kept saying leaders needed to change and adjust, but from what? Axel was saying that to manage diverse teams, yes, it was necessary to adjust, but you had to first know what you were adjusting from. As the adage goes, "if you can measure it, you can manage it."[1] Understand the behavior. Measure it, then manage it. Over the years, I had observed my own traits. I was competitive but that sometimes made me come across as pushy and selfish. I liked solving problems but often avoided having difficult conversations. I was direct and expected people to understand their job and get on with it with little management. My personal strengths and weaknesses list grew over the years, but Axel used a framework that made this easy for anyone to quickly create a profile for themselves and those around them.

Axel liked DISC.* This behavioral profiling model was quick, simple, and had been around for a number of decades. Many similar tests had been built off its core framework since the mid-20th century when the tests went to market. I had been through a few personality tests earlier in my career, and maybe it was the weak explanation regarding the tests' validity, but they always left me skeptical. My desperation to fix my work situation overrode these past bad experiences. I was willing to try anything to figure out how to get my team to make more phone calls.

Sunburned and dehydrated, I listened to Axel dissect the benefits of behavioral profiling tests that most organizations seemed to miss. The Muay Thai dwarf fighting continued in the background and the bar girls left us alone. Class was in session.

"We were taught the Golden Rule growing up: *Treat people the way you want to be treated*, but that is garbage." He paused to let this comment sink in. "The real answer is to treat people the way *they* want to be treated."

This idea was critical. People were different. Understand what makes them tick and treat them how they want to be treated, not how you want to be treated. They will like you more for it. I liked to work on my own and assumed others did too. Assumptions like these led to problems. Treating people the way they want to be treated was simple, profound and, unfortunately, difficult to do.

DISC focused on four different behavioral traits. Although people behave differently depending on the situation (a Centurion didn't act like a Centurion in front of his dear mother, hopefully), people tend to have behaviors that are, for the most part, predictable, especially when under pressure.

---

* Drawing on the earlier work of psychologist William Moulton Marston, industrial psychologist Walter Vernon Clarke developed the DISC behavioral assessment tool in the 1960s. In the 1970s, John Geier published the Personal Profile System®, an assessment based on Marston and Clarke's ideas.

DISC identified four types of personalities that helps explain behavior: DOMINANT, INFLUENCER, STEADY, and CAUTIOUS. There were other descriptors for each of these four buckets, but these were some of the most common. These traits exist as a spectrum from high to low, and each type included both positive and negative traits. People typically possess elements of all four, but everyone has their own unique combination of the four. Here is a quick overview:

Dominant

First up was D, or Dominant. People who score high on D are competitive and decisive. They are risks and make decisions based on their gut instinct. They love competition. They love winning. They love concise statements.

Strong D personalities can also come across as pushy, too aggressive, or cold—but Ds might not see any of these qualities as a bad thing. Famous D personalities include Jack Welch, Margaret Thatcher, Lee Kuan Yew, and Madonna. Most CEOs fall under this category.

D's fear a loss of control. They like to know (or think) they're in charge and easily get upset when they don't get their way. D's have already skipped ahead to the next section of this chapter, because they can't believe anyone would not want to possess these traits all the time.

Influencer

I stands for Influencer. People who are high Influencers are the social butterflies, the people who aren't afraid to talk to strangers at an event or in a bar. They love talking about ideas as well as themselves. They, like D's, are big-picture thinkers and have high amounts of energy and enthusiasm. On the downside, Influencers have the habit of being disorganized and easily distracted. Bill Clinton, Imelda Marcos, Richard Branson, and Oprah Winfrey are notable high I's.

I's can get distracted easily and don't always follow up on what they commit to doing.

Steady

S stands for "steady." These are people whose traits including being calm and patient. They are careful, family focused, and modest. They are considered trustworthy. It's no surprise that some of the most recognizable newscasters, back when news was news and not entertainment, were in this group. S's are generally quiet and will let others take the lead, whether it's during a conversation or in making a big decision. They seek consensus and don't like to rock the boat. Some well-known S personality types include Tom Hanks, Gandhi, Princess Diana, and our very own Mr. Asshole.

Cautious

The final profile type is C, which stands for "cautious." High C's are logical, precise, and formal. They are often engineers or accountants. They are the kind of people who read instructions and who actually know what they are talking about when it comes to topics that interest them. Mr. Spock from *Star Trek*, Roger Federer, Angela Merkel, Einstein and Alan Greenspan are all considered C's. Serial killers have been known to show strong tendencies toward this profile. Don't upset a C.

The system is often represented as four-boxes stacked into a square. D and S are positioned at opposite diagonal ends. The same goes with I and C. This is deliberate, because these personality descriptors are essentially opposite. In fact, they're so different that juxtaposing D's with S's or I's and C's is a tried-and-true sitcom formula. This is the buddy cop formula where two characters meet, initially can't stand each other, and while overcoming near impossible odds, learn that the differences that separate them are the very things that will make them succeed. The 21st century's global business story may very well be running through this movie script. How often do clashing personality types make a mess of a work situation? Where a quiet and reserved person has to get something from a demanding and hard-charging colleague? The quiet colleague may try to avoid conflict at all costs, which only frustrates the demanding counterpart who believes a direct approach, even if unpleasant, is more effective? The two don't see eye-to-eye, and the different approaches to handling the problem make them even less likely to want to work together. Their natural behavior styles make relationships worse.

There was no right and wrong or good and bad on a DISC profile. The problems came when people failed to realize that not everyone thinks the same way they do. Understanding one's own profile and the profile of people they work with is a giant step toward understanding people and being understood. When DISC profiling is used effectively, team dynamics can evolve, which makes communication, especially difficult topics, easier.

Many people put on a personality mask at work and play the character they think they are supposed to be. For example C's may appear to behave like D's. But the idea is that when pressure mounts and situations get tense, people shed their masks and their true natures come out. I was thinking about my work relationships. I would try and be friendly to my project manager, but when we were behind schedule, I was guilty of throwing all pleasantries aside and driving for immediate answers. It wasn't getting me the results I wanted.

How to treat people the way they want to be treated

I had all these customers and colleagues I had never met, but with whom I was communicating day in and day out. This was the new reality of working globally. By using DISC and models like it, it gave me a starting point to better understand why people behave the way they do. It helped me define the behaviors I was looking for when hiring, as well as what to avoid. I used it to help understand what motivated customers. It also helped me check myself and better understand how I was often part of the problem. This was a big piece of the puzzle.

Axel used the DISC model to understand people on this team, and he used it in other ways too. My first field lesson happened the morning after the Muay Thai experience. Here, he taught me how to profile other Centurions and then how to ruin their golf games. Once I figured this out, I could apply it in the real world.

"People leak their styles," he said cryptically.

I became Axel's behavioral psychology protégé. We profiled. We manipulated. Based on observations, we would assess each Centurion and get into the heads of our golf opponents with the goal of messing up their game even more than the free-flowing alcohol. It was noted, for example, that Lord Mort took pride in his new golf clubs. He always placed them in a special order in his bag, which was immaculate. He was detail-oriented, an ex-military IT security executive. Not surprisingly, he was the one who organized many of the outings. Clearly C tendencies at work here. Possibly a serial killer. How to mess with a C? Simply rearrange his clubs in between shots. Pay his caddie a few bucks to keep quiet, then watch the fireworks.

Roger Staddon, our naked friend, not surprisingly was outgoing and, to some, entertaining. He was also unorganized and paid little attention to detail. A high I. As he'd walk to his ball, we'd ask him what time it was or what time the flight was leaving to take us back to Singapore.

"How in the hell should I know, mate?"

Whiff. The ball would land 10 meters up the rough.

"Why in bloody hell don't you ask Mort? I don't even have a watch, you wanker!" He'd slam his club on the ground.

Mort would pipe up while rearranging his clubs. "Mate, the bus takes us to the airport at 3 for a 5 p.m. flight."

Axel and I would giggle like idiots.

These profiling models probably weren't meant to take advantage of people, but there's something about the Centurions that inevitably led us to the dark side even with a tool like DISC.

How to adjust at work

DISC became a core implement to helping me to cut through the complexity of doing business across the world. As tools go, it was blunt and didn't work miracles, but it helped clarify the challenges I was up against. Why was I not selling as well as when I was in the United States or Europe? Why were my salespeople not working out? Why was I not getting along with this person I was working with remotely?

Axel required all his managers to take this test and to share the results with the rest of the team. By exchanging their profiles, each employee could get a chance to see everyone else's likes and dislikes. This gave the team a common language to describe behaviors, which was especially helpful in teams where English was not everyone's first language. It was also a safer way to have difficult conversations about an individual's gaps. "It's not me saying you aren't doing this, but the test suggests this could be a problem." It was a soft way to work on improving communication skills that were so desperately needed across organizations.

The tools in the hands of someone like Axel helped bring people with wildly diverse backgrounds together and get them to overcome their differences.

"Treat people the way *they* want to be treated," Axel kept repeating as he wrapped a condom over Lord Mort's three wood golf club. The losing team paid for a bottle of vodka, and Axel's tampering would surely set Mort over the edge.

Back in the working world, there were plenty of examples of how Axel treated people the way they wanted to be treated:

Some people don't speak up in meetings (S's or C's). It was common for more dominant types (D's or I's) to monopolize discussions. Over time, this could lead to real problems, where the quiet person felt like they weren't being heard, and the more talkative person thought the quiet person had nothing to contribute. Trust would evaporate.

A common response was to tell the quiet people that they need to speak up. But does that ever work?

Axel would instead spend time one on one explaining the importance of getting everyone to participate. He would coach the quiet person before a meeting or conference call and give them a specific item they would be required to bring up. In these mini-coaching sessions, he made it easier for that person to speak up. He would say to his quiet S teammate before the meeting, "You know a lot about this topic, so when this item comes up, I am going to ask you to share a few thoughts. If you would like, we can go through those now so you're comfortable with them for the call." He created safety for those who performed better in safe environments.

For the dominant types, he did the opposite. "Shut the hell up so the others can talk," he would bark at a D type. Then he'd stroke their ego a bit by adding, "and I want you to wrap up the meeting by summarizing what's been discussed since I know you know this topic inside and out." He would give the highly competitive Ds little wins every step along the way to keep them happy and engaged.

He did these things subtly. Only by understanding the framework could someone catch him in the act. He'd tell strong I types, "Let's grab a drink so I can hear your opinions on this." With C types, he'd approach the same situation by saying, "Spend a few days looking at the data and get back to me with a list of options." In other words, let the talkers talk and let the analysts analyze.

"The challenge you have," he told me, "is that you have hired a lot of S and C behavior types. People who were generally more quiet, steady, and family oriented. They don't like confrontation."

Esses and Sees! It was starting to make sense. I had hired people who were way out of their comfort zone making cold calls. The sales backgrounds they had in the past were focused on nurturing existing relationships, not calling strangers day in and day out.

He was right. Not only had I come in with a business model built in, and for, Western markets, I had been hiring people who were an unnatural fit.

On average, cold calling resulted in one phone call out of a hundred ending with a legitimate potential sale. That's a 99 percent rejection rate. An S or C personality didn't take rejection well. But, if someone who was a high D got rejected, they'd get mad. They'd want to win. *How dare someone say no to me? What an idiot. Next.*

So I sat down with Jing Yi when I got back to the office and we went through DISC together. Unsurprisingly we were polar opposites. Together we rewrote a hiring approach. I wanted competitors, athletes, and people who have taken on big challenges like mountain climbing or skiing (hard to find at the equator). Musicians were another group that worked. People who were comfortable performing in front of others, people who could hear patterns and improvise accordingly. These high "I" traits turned out to be great in a sales setting.

We built a plan to coach our current batch of callers, helping them find ways to break out of their comfort zones and develop more confidence when talking on the phones. Jing Yi would take the lead on this new coaching approach. I left the office that night and headed back to the airport for a client project. I felt like we had really taken a big leap forward.

This is the part of any business case study where I am supposed to conclude by saying the plan worked. Well, it didn't. Jing Yi quit the next morning. She did it by text. She said the callers wouldn't listen to her and that only I could coach them because I was the boss.

Dammit.

I needed D's and I's. So I went back to get Axel's advice.

"D's and I's are hard to find in Asia, my friend," he declared.

Axel wasn't just throwing out stereotypes here. Models like DISC were being used to look not only at individual traits but at the cultural level as well. The United States and Australia were cultures that could be generalized as being outgoing, independent, and comfortable with risk taking. These were D / I characteristics. Latin America and India were more expressive I types. Singapore and China were considered steady, focusing on values such as the importance of the group, family traditions, order, respect for seniority, and not rocking the boat. Singapore, in fact, sat directly in between S and C traits, the exact opposite of what I was looking for. Germany, the UK, and Japan leaned more toward careful, task-focused C characteristics.[2] This profiling model painted a high-level overview of several cultural traits.

I soon found a new project manager and tried again. This time, we started with the behavioral profile and we turned that into the foundation for how we would work together. "I think we're having one of those 'moments'" was our coded way of saying one of us had just completely misunderstood the other. It was a great way to bridge our working styles.

DISC led to a big aha moment for two reasons. First, it explained why I was having trouble filling my call center with D's and I's. They were hard to find in a culture that didn't place the same value around many of those aggressive traits I wanted. Second, I started thinking about Western companies and how they were expanding into Asia. When a company wanted to open an office in a new market, who did they send? Someone who was demanding, fearless, and focused on results. Someone who was willing to leave their family and friends to make the move. Risk takers. And where were they moving to over the past few decades? To growth markets, places like Singapore—where traits of harmony, consistency, safety, and putting family first define the country's value system. This is in fact the case for most of southeast Asia and China. D's and I's going to the land of S's and C's. If not acknowledged and addressed, it was a classic mismatch. I will do a deep dive into one such mismatch in the next chapter.

The lesson here was that while the cultural data sets and regional differences were important, people were unique with their own likes and dislikes. In order to get things done, individual personalities had to be considered. Yes, it was important to adapt to the part of the world you were working in, but it was just as important to adapt to the individuals you worked with. Leaders needed high levels of self-awareness in order to manage teams, especially diverse or remote teams. They needed to understand their strengths and weaknesses, so they could adapt to whatever situation they found themselves in. Behavioral profiling tests were a great way to get started.

Survival Guide Tips:

- ✔ To enhance relationships, *treat people the way they want to be treated.* Adjust what you say and how you say it. The future of globalization is *human.*

- ✔ Take time to study peoples' behaviors to understand their motivations. People leak their styles. Tailor your messaging to ensure people hear what you need them to hear.

- ✔ Behavioral profiling tools can help in understanding your own communication styles as well as others.

Chapter 6

Claire the Bulldog

"Yesterday I was clever, so I wanted to change the world. Today I am wise, so I am changing myself."

—*Rumi, 13th-century Persian poet*

Opening offices in new parts of the world and growing global teams can go wrong in so many ways. Even if you import a proven performer like Claire who has a bulldog's tenacity. Here's her story and advice on how to overcome the pitfalls she encountered.

OUT OF THE blue, Texas Joe—the original *slap dragon*—reconnected with me.

"Our business in Singapore keeps growing, so we're taking the next step," Joe told me in his Texas drawl.

His business was *growing*? Did that first campaign with the dragons actually work?

"That campaign of yours didn't do shit. My initial project is growing, but we need someone out there, so we decided to open an office. I'm sending someone and I want you two to team up to bring in more business. None of this bullshit like last time, though. Now you'll have to work for my money." He laughed.

His expansion plan wasn't at all unusual. Businesses across industries like his frequently won a first deal somewhere in a new region through either a global arrangement or referral. That was enough to justify the expansion. Growth was addictive, and in Joe's case, investors were already sold on Asia, because it seemed like everyone else was expanding there. That was enough to convince smart people to write big checks.

How does a company choose who opens an office in a new market? What traits does that person need in order to make things work? What traits should be avoided? One lesson had become clear: leaders needed to accept that they didn't know what they didn't know. The faster someone got past that, the faster they could begin to adjust to uncertain situations. Sadly, organizations around the world kept repeating mistakes at this stage either by selecting the wrong person or someone who was so set in his or her ways they were unable to make the business work. It appeared that Texas Joe was about to make one of these mistakes.

Actually, Joe had more market intelligence than others because he hired my company a year earlier to speak to a number of prospects and try to bring in some new deals. No one was interested and we knew why. It turned out, companies in Malaysia, Singapore and

Hong Kong were ignoring Texas Joe because local competitors were offering the same services for less. They also had local teams who were taking care of their accounts. Why pay more for a company on the other side of the world? He did not like what my team had told him about the local conditions, so he fired me the first time. Joe and his management team knew shockingly little about the region, the different cities, histories, languages, and rules of law. All he knew was that a bank in Singapore had bought his software and that there were a lot more banks in Asia growing like crazy.

On that last point, he was right. Known as the "Switzerland of Asia," Singapore's financial sector was growing like crazy. As the West staggered out of the global financial crisis, between 2008 and 2012 Singapore's financial services industry grew 163 percent.[1] Switzerland's long banking tradition of client anonymity was under attack as the US government started forcing Swiss banks to share details of their US clients' activities. Singapore wasn't under the same scrutiny. Their banks had retained the strict laws protecting anonymity and became a logical alternative. With the growing wealth being created, and sometimes pilfered, across the region and landing in Singapore some industry experts have predicted that Singapore may one day overtake Switzerland as the world's largest hub of offshore wealth.[2] These banks needed more infrastructure, security, and customer support. Software companies like Joe's lined up to try to help spend their newfound riches.

Joe paid attention to these impressive growth trends but completely ignored the information we had given him about the strong local competition. He had decided to expand to Asia anyway.

So, how does a company choose who should open their office in a foreign country? The decision is critical because this individual will be the face of the company, the brand ambassador, the person responsible for setting a foundation in new markets, and for maintaining the company culture. Given the irrational growth expectations, the role was enormous.

What characteristics do companies look for? Obviously, someone who understands the business and who's assertive enough to fight through all the uncertainties of foreign markets. Someone independent enough to operate alone far from home but at the same time loyal and trustworthy to the company. Stepping up to move to the other side of the world is risky for everyone involved. Seasoned executives with a lot of experience usually make the shortlist but often don't want to uproot their families. Younger executives are eager to take on the new responsibilities but lack experience and bring added risk into an already risky venture. So, who goes?

Every case is different, but it is often the risk takers, the dominant personalities, who take the offer. This is precisely why Texas Joe chose Claire.

"She's a bulldog, a real nut cutter."

"Did he say, "nut cutter"? I crossed my legs. She's young and aggressive. Perfect for whipping Asia into shape for us."

"Sounds like it," I agreed. And I did agree. A leader has to be tough enough to make things work in unfamiliar markets. I was still trying to process all the new lessons I had picked up from Jake the Snake and the Centurions over the past few months. A part of me knew that I should question my instincts when it came to leadership qualities, but because I was still fairly new to the region, I hadn't gotten to the point where I could apply this in a real-world situation. I was still thinking like I would back home.

Companies can expand into new markets in two ways. They can partner with someone already in the region to act as their representative, or they can open an office themselves. The option to partner can range from loose agreements to joint ventures to going all the way and buying a local business. This is where things start getting complicated. Every country has different rules, and those rules tend to change based on economic and political climates. Some countries have laws in place designed to protect locals from foreigners taking over. Some require a local citizen to maintain majority ownership. There are workarounds to most of these rules, but those workarounds cost money and time.

Countries can also change the rules on foreigners whenever they want. A universal response in times of trouble, when an economy slows down or overheats, is to blame people from the outside. Foreigners are always in the crosshairs when things go wrong. A few years later, I would learn this the hard way (which will be explained later).

Companies looked to mitigate these types of risks as best they could. The safest way to grow overseas was to do it yourself, which is what Texas Joe did. He had his one Asian client, his funding and his bulldog. He was ready to open an office.

Sometimes called a "greenfield start" because of the supposedly untapped markets, opening an office overseas provides the most control, or at least the illusion of control. Control usually comes with a downside, and in this case the downside was that things took longer to get up and running. And most companies were coming to growth markets for short-term wins whether they were willing to admit it or not. Investors expected quick results.

Naturally, I began referring to Texas Joe's bulldog as Claire *Greenfield*. With a master's degree from Texas A&M University, Claire was the number one sales rep for Joe's software company for four years running. She was confident and sociable. Having begun her career in various project management roles, Claire had learned how to run groups and hit targets. But, watching her paycheck remain unchanged month in and month out, she soon became restless. She wanted more money, more responsibility, more wins—and, really, she wanted more control. Claire was the master of her own destiny and believed the world was meant for people like her to reshape it into whatever got results. If there wasn't a path forward, she'd make one. Beneath the surface of her Southern charisma was an unmistakable ambition. Claire was not to be messed with. She was kinetic. Joe was right: she was a bulldog.

Even better, Claire the Bulldog had a husband who was being transferred by his large tech company over to Singapore on a coveted expat package. The company was moving the family, including two young children, across the planet. They gave them housing, a car, living allowance, club membership and paid for the kids' private education. Some lucky expat employees could still enjoy a traditional "hardship allowance" (additional pay given to people who live in developing countries or even war zones) for living in Singapore. *Slap dragon* companies with little understanding of Singapore applied hardship allowance and paid hundreds of thousands of dollars extra to incentivize employees to take a job. Grown men could be found lounging at their poolside bars injuring themselves from laughter because their companies thought Singapore was in China or Indonesia. The only danger was if an HR exec back home took 30 seconds to do an internet search on "Singapore" and cut off the hardship allowance. This kind of package was destined for extinction.

The point was, Texas Joe had hit the jackpot. His top choice to open his Asia business was going to do it heavily subsidized by a larger company—Claire's husband's.

Claire was clean-cut, attractive and didn't mess around. The first time I met her, she ignored my face completely and stared about an inch up my forehead and further through my skull like she was scanning my brain. She was either looking for me to help achieve her goals or a reason to move me out of her way. Like most aggressive salespeople, she understood the need for marketing—which I'd been rehired to help her with—but she just didn't like marketers. As a salesperson who sold marketing projects, I sympathized, partially, and this was probably why she didn't find me completely useless.

Claire had set up shop in what's called a "serviced office" under one of the largest providers of office space in the world. This was a working space with shared receptionists, meeting rooms, and kitchens. It was a common starting point for many overseas companies since it acted as a one-stop-shop to get things up and running. Today, the industry has expanded with more remote workers popping up all over the world.

Serviced offices had a few unwritten ground rules. First, they were expensive. When a market was growing like crazy, serviced office fees became ludicrous. You did NOT step into a conference room without permission, because the company you're visiting got charged for using the space. You did NOT get a drink from the stocked refrigerator.

Drink prices made hotel mini-bar rates look like bargains. The attentive secretaries were happy to mail or fax documents for you, or to help with administrative work, but it came with a hefty fee. At the time, these secretaries' hourly rates were over *three times* what I was billing for my people, and they kicked in the second you so much as even looked at them. I had one client who was billed $75 for asking a secretary to stamp and mail a letter.

Whenever I walked into Claire's serviced office, I froze when I heard the secretary ask, "May I help you?" I was afraid to answer in case Claire would be charged for being told I was there. "*Nut cutter,*" Texas Joe's voice echoed in my head.

"It's OK. I've texted—I've let her know I'm here. She'll probably come out, so you don't have to do anything." I didn't sit on the couch, didn't touch a newspaper. Waiting for Claire, I fantasized about billing clients for my senior employees at the same rates these entry-level administrative assistants charged.

I had been to the same place a year earlier visiting another company. Out of the six companies listed now, not one remained from the year before. How many had closed down? How many had succeeded and struck off to find bigger and cheaper office space? Governments around the region were tight lipped about these kinds of statistics even though they should be easy to track. Some companies would officially de-register local entities, but it took time and money to get this done. Many simply left town, making statistics on failure rates tricky. An office tower in Shanghai, well known for housing foreign companies, unintentionally developed a reputation as a cemetery for foreign businesses when they changed their directory to electronic screens because so many companies kept closing. Previously, every time a new company rented an office, they had to make their business sign for the lobby entrance. The problem was the signs hadn't even dried before the companies shut down. Electric signs were faster to go live and, more important, faster to delete. For companies, the message was clear: chances of survival in this market were slim and everyone was a click of a mouse away from being deleted.

Claire darted out from around a corner, hand outstretched. We always started with a brusque handshake. "This place is filled with idiots" was how I was greeted. We were within earshot of the front desk. "You need to meet the sales guy I just hired. He's going to be following up on the leads you get."

"Sounds good." It didn't. It sounded ominous.

The odd couple

The office was comically small. It was like a walk-in closet with two desks, two chairs and a narrow window with a view of another nearby building. There was nothing on the walls except a white board containing sales targets on one column and actual sales on the other. The "actual sales" was blank. Sitting meekly at his desk below the board was the new sales guy, Lionel Chen. Claire squeezed through the small gap between the two desks, sat down, and glared first at Lionel, and then at the blank whiteboard, and then back at Lionel. Claire was as direct, highly-strung, and demanding as it got. Poor Lionel Chen. He had no idea what he was in for. After four years selling software from a giant multinational, Lionel happened to have the coveted Rolodex: a who's-who of potential local software buyers. In the right hands, those names and numbers were the key to making a killing, and Claire knew it. Even though he was a head taller than Claire, her physical presence eclipsed her new employee. He half stood up to greet me with a limp, damp handshake. "I'm Lionel," he said, staring at my neck and avoiding eye contact.

This man was on death row. He did not stand a chance working for the Bulldog. She hired his résumé and his contact list and had convinced herself she could turn him into what she wanted—a sales hunter. From what I could see, Lionel was the reverse. Although I was still getting my head around the personality systems Axel had shown me, Lionel appeared to be the opposite of his boss. And yet here he was, crammed into a tiny, expensive closet with a woman on the verge of violence. He smiled nervously and gave one-word answers whenever he could get away with it. Clearly, this was going to be a problem.

Not only were they opposite personality types, they came from very different cultures, which in this case only seemed to make things even more uncomfortable. After giving Lionel a quick overview of the products, she sent him out to hunt and bring her deals. She expected him to know what to do and it seemed like Lionel had expected more details than this. This situation was a train wreck in the making, but the reason I didn't try to help is because it was so common across the region, it seemed like this was just the way things were done: aggressive Western managers at odds with their local staff. I had gone through it myself with my project manager, Jing Yi. At this point, I was just beginning to change my working style by using Axel's advice. This serviced office should have invested in one of those electronic signboards.

Lionel had graduated from one of Singapore's top universities in the middle of his class with a degree in engineering, and then worked his way through several jobs at mid- to large-size companies. His résumé told a common Singaporean story of a twenty-something slowly climbing up the corporate ladder and eventually settling for a four-year stint at a well-known software company as a vaguely titled account manager.

When asked what that role involved, he responded, "I, you know, managed accounts."

The question on my mind was: *Why did he leave such a safe role and join a risky start-up?*

Lionel lived with his parents and younger sister in one of the million or so HDB flats (Housing Development Buildings) on the island, where over 80 percent of Singaporeans reside. The family owned their three-bedroom unit. A maid also lived with them. That's five adults in less than 1,300 square feet. As property prices continued to spike, valuations of some of these government-built units were worth three-quarters of a million dollars or more. Most Singaporeans owned at least one such unit outright because they were sold by the government decades earlier at attractive prices.

Because he lived with his family and a maid who cooked, cleaned, and did the laundry, Lionel had never paid a rent check or a utility bill in his life. But he had bought his own car, which was where a big chunk of his earnings went. "Singaporeans have expenses, they're just different than yours," he said to me later, on one of the few occasions we chatted about non-work.

His Honda Civic was a few years old but, aside from lacking that familiar new car smell, no one would know it. It was immaculate. As of 2019, a new Honda Civic in the United States cost around $20,000. The same car in Singapore came in around $100,000. Most of the $80,000 difference ended up in the government's piggy bank in the form of taxes. Cars on the island state, like many other parts of locals' lives, were closely controlled. The advantages were less congestion and cleaner air; the disadvantages included paying six figures for a Honda Civic.

Lionel's story was not unique. Most Singaporeans moved back in with their families after graduating. They did this until they got married, at which time the newlywed couple moved in with one of the families. Through birth, marriage, and death, the family unit remained as a tightly woven network. This was common across the region. In cultures with strong Chinese influence, family takes precedence.

This difference in family living situations from the West was an example of how some overseas products needed to adjust if they wanted to be locally relevant. One business offering well-being and nutritional advice for employees at Fortune 500 companies was confounded when trying to expand across Asia. This US company's software included daily lifestyle recommendations, including walking more by parking a car further from office buildings, cutting down on bread and other dietary ideas, and helping people who lived on their own eat healthier. Their expansion plan was based on diabetes trends within a population, which was a good start, but the market researchers didn't complete their homework. Theirs was a solution designed to solve problems in Western lifestyles, not other parts of the world. The software did not consider the fact that cars are not as ubiquitous as in the US or that large parts of the world had a rice-based diet rather than bread-based and that twenty-somethings didn't typically live on their own after graduating from university. Unhealthy lifestyles were universal, but how people became unhealthy varied considerably and could not be solved with a single set of recommendations. Instead of researching and customizing, the company invested in expanding a sales and marketing team only to find themselves promoting a product irrelevant to these new markets.

Lionel was generally quiet around me, and I sensed he felt I was more on Claire's side than his. He was right. I didn't think he could last long in Claire's world. I just hoped he gave us his contact list and went away before Claire ripped his face off. Our one real conversation happened when he drove us to a prospect meeting one morning. I had been asked to tag along and spy on him.

It was during this drive that Lionel confided he was looking for a girlfriend, and his mother was pressuring him to find a wife. Although he said he wanted a relationship, it didn't seem like his heart was in it. He also admitted his mother wanted him to start his own business, and that's why he had taken the job with Claire—for the experience. What kind of business did he want to start? He didn't know.

I asked him if he thought the sales targets given to him by Claire were fair. He says they were okay and that he could hit them. Again, like his approach to the idea of dating, his heart didn't seem in it. "The targets should be pretty okay *lah*." After a pause he added, "I need time." The phrase *lah* in Singapore and Malaysia is one of the mainstays of the local dialect. It's sort of a filler word, the way teenagers say "like" after every few words, but it has more nuance than a space filler. *Lah* is meant to lighten the statement. It softens the agreement and puts a hedge into any commitment.

"Do you think you can achieve this sales target?"

"Can *lah*."

It was more like saying, "I'll try." That could mean a lot of things.

What it didn't seem to mean was *yes* or that it will even necessarily be attempted. "Can, *lah*" made Claire's blood pressure spike.

We arrived five minutes late, which was considered on time. "You're not a stickler for time, are you, Lionel?" I said sarcastically, testing my cultural communication skills.

"We're okay," he answered, not understanding the hint. Time, as I remembered from Jake's call center work, was relative. It was ill advised to show up five minutes late to a meeting in Zurich, in fact it might be advisable to apologize for not arriving early. In Poland, the national rail service announced a train was "on time" if it arrived within a six-minute window. In Japan, conductors have been known to write letters of apology if their train arrives 60 seconds late. Time-sensitive businesspeople around the globe continue to be mystified by their time-flexible counterparts and vice-versa.

We arrived at the meeting and were made to wait for nearly 20 minutes in a conference room. Lionel was done talking. He pecked away at his phone and, through a reflection off a glass wall behind him, I could see he was playing a game involving bits of candy floating around the screen.

The meeting was awful. Lionel spoke to the IT director of the bank about whatever it was he is supposed to sell in a soft monotone and didn't ask one question of the prospect. It seemed Lionel already knew this was not going to turn into a sale, and the prospect already knew he wasn't going to buy what Lionel was selling. And yet, everyone remained in character as if directed by some hidden puppet master. The meeting ended by agreeing on some noncommittal next steps ("can, *lah*")—but it was clear there would be no follow-up.

A failure to communicate

Singaporeans raise their kids to win. It is no coincidence their students continue to have some of the highest test scores in the world. A 2016 OECD report ranked Singapore as having the highest math and science scores for teenagers out of 76 countries reviewed.[3] The runners-up included Hong Kong, South Korea, Japan, and Taiwan, with Finland snatching the sixth spot, the first Western country to make the list. The United States placed twenty-sixth.

The pressure to have the right answers could be extreme. The tight family relationships, right down to multiple generations living under the same roof, reinforce this pressure to succeed. It's hard to hide when your family is staring at you in a cramped living room.

As countries go, Singapore was a start-up. And a wildly successful one at that. Officially established in 1965, the founding fathers (actually, only one, a man named Lee Kuan Yew) acted quickly and decisively (dominantly) to turn the ex-British colony into the regional powerhouse it is today. Like an overbearing parent, the new nation's leadership expected nothing less than obedience and success from its children, and in exchange the country would get rich. This basically worked. The Asian Tiger quickly rocketed past its neighbors.

But pressure to succeed created unexpected downsides. One being a desire not to fail. Ever. Risk, therefore, was something to avoid. You cannot fail at something if you don't try in the first place. Lionel Chen embodied this success-failure paradox. He had not been raised to work in the type of entrepreneurial setting Claire had set up. He had done everything he was supposed to do all his life—good grades, decent jobs, family loyalty. He saw Claire's company as a chance to raise himself to a new level of success, a chance to win, and he went for it without understanding the levels of independence required to succeed in an unstructured environment. Representing a new product in a market meant facing a lot of rejection and a lot of risk.

Claire gave Lionel six months to prove himself—in reality, that meant three. Even with his local expertise and relevant contacts, Claire suffered from buyer's remorse immediately.

"I'm giving him the benefit of the doubt here, but I've been in the same room with him for the last six hours and he hasn't picked up the goddamned phone once," she confided one afternoon over coffee at

Starbucks, where the drinks were cheaper than at her office. "I've asked him for his sales plan, and he says he's working on it. He keeps saying he's doing research and needs to learn more about our products. I just need him to get me in front of his damn contacts, yesterday."

I had never seen anyone drink a cup of black coffee as fast as Claire. It was official: I was impressed. Terrified, but impressed.

"Get him to give you his sales plan and his list of prospects and start setting weekly targets," I advised, not following Axel's earlier advice of adjusting. "Make it clear this is time sensitive. Push him."

"Don't worry about that."

I wasn't.

Claire fired Lionel exactly 90 days after he started. He was given a two-month severance. Since the serviced office controlled all phone lines and charged huge rates for calls, even local calls, the monthly bill showed that Lionel had picked up the phone fifteen times during his three-month stint. When Claire got access to his company laptop, she saw he had sent emails to no one outside the company. "He said he was emailing his contacts through his personal email address because that's how things are done here," she said. "That's bullshit, right?"

We were back at our usual coffee shop where dark tropical clouds were quickly forming outside. My coffee was too hot to drink. Hers was empty.

"Yes, it is."

Claire used the same playbook that had worked so well for her back in Texas. She was confrontational because that's how she was used to getting things done. Fight it out, figure it out, and move on. With Claire, there were no drawn-out lunches spent socializing or discussing any topics other than work. In fact, unless you were hitting your number, you shouldn't be wasting time with lunch at all. Eat lunch at your desk—don't disappear for an hour or more.

Unfortunately, this was the worst way to manage someone like Lionel, who considered Claire's direct speaking style not only intimidating but rude. He had no idea how to respond because he wasn't used to it. So he said nothing. In fact, he took longer lunch breaks just to avoid the pressure at the office. As far as Lionel was concerned, Claire was not to be trusted because she showed no interest in his life outside work and seemed to only confide in other Westerners like me. Lionel stuck with the playbook he was familiar with and remained quiet.

Silence to someone like Claire was the worst kind of response. She wanted confirmation in the form of agreement or, hell, someone to fight back. Claire missed having loud arguments in the workplace, and Lionel's lack of response pushed her to become even more direct and aggressive. Their natural behavior ended up pushing each other further away. It was a complete misalignment.

$2,200 per phone call

Claire ran the numbers. Based on the salary she paid out and the actual work done, she had compensated Lionel around $2,200 dollars per phone call.

"He was the best one who came through my door," she said, not really to me, not really to anyone. "How in the hell am I going to make this work?"

Of course, she did not give up. Claire immediately interviewed new candidates. This time she chose someone closer to her own personality. She hired an Australian new to the region who was everything Lionel was not: smooth talking, outwardly confident, and completely lacking in industry experience. His lack of relationships in key accounts combined with his slightly cocky attitude failed to win over prospects. Three months later he was gone.

Claire decided to put a pause on hiring and instead handled the selling on her own, which went well but left her unable to focus on other areas of growing the region.

My company was still helping her generate leads, albeit with little results to show for.

About a year into her Asian adventure, I met up with Claire and talked about the lessons learned. "If I could do it all over again, I'd slow down everything. I think Lionel might have worked out had I brought him onboard in a more deliberate and steady way rather than throwing him into the deep end. My management approach in the US was basically to assume the team had what they needed and they would come to me if they needed something. He wasn't comfortable doing that, and I blamed him for it." She had switched from black coffee to chamomile tea in another attempt to dial down her intensity. "But when it comes to working with the team back home"—her old fire came back—"I would have pushed like hell to get small changes made so that our software made sense for local companies here." Claire had discovered a global leadership approach that included using her bulldog-like strengths when dealing with her team back in the US and then massively adjusting when dealing with her team in different regions. Black coffee in some situations, decaf tea in others.

Would Texas Joe have gone for it? "I would have insisted he fly out to talk with local clients and prospects." She smiled and added, "I would have had your friend Smitty take him to that lady-boy bar he always talks about."

Would these changes have saved the business? Would they have made Lionel a success? It certainly would have improved their chances. Claire had figured things out too late, and now she needed to decide if she was going to hire yet another sales rep and try again.

Claire's problems and the way she tried to solve them mirrored my own, and observing her helped me see how important it was to adapt. I had lost my project manager Jing Yu because of similar issues. I managed to hire a few new people and made more of an effort to adjust my management approach by treating each person the way they wanted to be treated. I was seeing slow progress. However, finding enough of the right people who could handle a high level of rejection was hard. In a country filled with people who have never failed, what I was attempting seemed insurmountable. People taking these jobs were drawn in by the allure of a start-up but then paralyzed by the risks. Like Claire, I continued searching for answers.

Survival Guide Tips:

✔ To build strong teams, manage diversity openly. Ignoring diversity can be disastrous for teams. Actively managed diversity can be the foundation for powerful cooperation.

✔ Adapting behaviors sounds easy but requires a strategy. Plan and rehearse before important interactions.

Chapter 7

Survival Kit:
When Confucius Skypes Socrates

"The oldest, shortest words—yes and no—are those which require the most thought."

—*Pythagoras*

Five thousand years of cultural differences discussed over a few pints helps provide added context to the diverse working styles across the world. We have seen examples of when these differences are misunderstood, they become liabilities. A global survival kit can turn differences into assets.

DESPITE THE challenges of hiring the right people, business improved and many of my clients were happy. It seemed as if there was an endless supply of Western companies eager to break into Asia, and my team and I were on the ground to get their sales and marketing up and running. With the cross-cultural datasets and behavioral profiling models, I was getting the hang of things, but I was still a long way from really knowing how to apply these tools in a consistent way. While I had started to figure out how to run effective teams in Singapore and manage remote workers around the region, it was still a challenge getting the clients in the US, UK or Australia to understand how they should be adapting to local conditions. To achieve this level of understanding, I needed a better way to explain these differences in how business gets done effectively around the world.

India, China, the Middle East—my passport bulged with added pages and scraped-off visa stickers to make way for new ones.[1] During one such trip, I found myself in Taipei, Taiwan, with Chen, an IT reseller and curious character. This meant he resold other companies' stuff. If a company makes a security software or internet router, he would add it to his product list and seek out buyers within his territory. I had been asked to get Chen to resell one of my client's security servers. I was a middleman hired to find a middleman.

Medium height and skinny, Chen looked tense and intense. I guessed his age to be around 30, but he was closer to 50. Always moving, he had nervous eyes that made him look happy and angry at the same time; a near constant Cheshire cat smile curled his lips. He was a self-described "optimistic skeptic."

"China made me that way," he said, pointing to a wall that I assumed was the direction of China, which was just over 100 miles to the west. "That place has the most amazing potential, but man is their system messed up." Growing up in the geopolitical hotspot that is Taiwan seemed to give Chen some of his edginess, even though he was enjoying the recent economic growth. It was as if he was experiencing two opposite emotions at the same time. He was slightly unsettling until you got to you know him.

Growing up in a wealthy family outside of Taipei, he moved to California to get a degree at UCLA. He didn't say what kind of degree or where the family money came from. But his years in the States showed immediately in some of his mannerisms and how he spoke. He was more direct and outwardly opinionated than anyone I had met in Taiwan. His distrust of China was evident. "I've got a go-bag, you know, a survival kit for when the mainlanders come over for an *extended visit*. This thing has everything I need. I can disappear, fast."

This was off to an awkward start. Later Chen explained that his survival kit was filled with a few items of clothes, a data storage device containing his key files, US dollars, euros, medicine, and small family heirlooms, some of which were hundreds of years old and were smuggled out of China in the 1940s. "Taiwan has more China history hidden in it than China," he said.

Our meeting was quick and to the point. He knew which products of mine he wanted and had already decided to add them to his portfolio before I got there. "I like working with Americans. You have meetings where you get right into the business." He found this very amusing and started signing my contract before we even sat down. He was doing his impression of how he thought meetings in American were run. "We could have done all of this over the phone but I'm in Taiwan, so you have to fly thousands of miles just to shake my hand. HA!"

This was annoying and I wanted to go home, but there was a part of me that was curious. Sometimes these trips turned into unexpected adventures.

"Let's get a drink. We can do that *guanxi* you Westerners always talk about." He opened his office door and disappeared down a drab, seemingly endless, office hallway.

"Follow me."

And so once again, I found myself on an early afternoon,

frustrated and confused about business plans, following another crazy character down an unknown rabbit hole.

Mustard and salt

Chen barked his order to a waitress without looking at her. Drinks arrived quickly. His behavior to me and the waitress couldn't have been more different. To me, he was friendly and good natured, to the waitress, it was as if she was less than human. "You need to learn about Confucius," he said out of the blue as he started ripping off small pieces of his drink coaster.

Oh no. Was this guy trying to convert me? Confucians don't have the same kind of missionary-like zeal as some Western religions, so thankfully, I was safe. But I wanted to see where this was going and had no other meetings for the day.

"You people (he meant Westerners) think you understand the idea of relationships over here, but you don't. It's not about meeting people and getting to know them," as he waved his arms indicating what the two of us were doing, "it's booshit."

His accent was wonderful.

"Relationships are more complex than that. We look at things differently. We *think* differently.[2] It goes all the way back to Confucius— *before* Confucius. But he's a good place to start since he at least wrote a lot of it down."

I started taking notes on my drink coaster, which gave Chen an idea. He got up and returned a moment later with a plastic bottle of mustard. Grabbing a saltshaker, he put them next to each other. "This," he said holding the saltshaker, "is the West. Because you're white. And this," the mustard, "is Asia. Because we're yellow. I'm a blend, he tapped the two together, "since I went to school in America. I'm a banana—yellow on the outside but white on the inside. A Twinkie! Get it?" I got it.

Before diving into Chen's mustard-salt lecture, it's worth considering what exactly the "West" or "Western" label means, especially as it relates to the "East," "Eastern" or even "Asian." The sun rises in the east, which is where we turn to *orient* ourselves. Living on a spherical planet tends to make this idea, from a geographic standpoint, confusing and arbitrary. On top of that, Australia is Western, but in the East. Even the term "Asia" was coined by Westerners. Who handed out all these labels anyway?

It turns out the Romans get credit for first using the "East" and "West" terms in a geopolitical sense. They decided anything beyond the Aegean Sea was in the east. This meant that, according to the Romans, the Greeks—the founders of Western civilization—were from the East.

Over time, the concept of East and West shifted from geographical to cultural. Where does Western culture start and end? Is Russia western? What about Latin America? It's not black and white. Or in Chen's case, salt and mustard.

"Western thought originated in Greece, right?" Chen asked rhetorically. Greece, being the center of Western ideas, located east of where the Roman *west* began. "What are the core principles of Greek thought? You know, Socrates, Plato, and Aristotle, that kind of booshit," pointing at the shaker, spilling salt on the table.

The Greeks developed methods of logical analysis to try to explain what they saw around them. They did this by separating objects from their surroundings. Observing those objects and then trying to understand how they fit into their larger systems. This was deductive reasoning.

All men are mortal.
Socrates is a man.
Therefore, Socrates is mortal.

Studying these objects, the Greeks made hypotheses. In some cases, they got down to the cellular level in their studies. They wanted to look at the smallest parts and see how they interacted with the larger whole. Smaller to bigger. The word *microbiology* comes from Greek. They looked at the pieces and asked why and searched for the answers. By breaking things apart and separating them, the Greeks believed they could understand how these parts made their larger systems work.

"And now," Chen picked up the mustard, "compare that to what Confucius was doing around the same time. Confucius was, like, *Why would someone separate a part from its greater whole?*" In other words, how can you understand something in isolation when it exists within a larger and more complex framework? "Shit's complex, man! If everything is interconnected, you can't break it apart, so you go about studying and thinking about it from that starting point." Confucius was asking *how* something exists in *relation* to the world around it.

I wrote "'how" not "why" on my coaster.

He shook the saltshaker at me. "You people don't like contradictions, but they exist everywhere. Western mindsets can't deal with contradictions when you've made nice and neat categories. You have to explain and rationalize everything, but you know you can't, right? That's why you guys are so crazy."

The Confucian mindset was comfortable with more than one truth existing at the same time. Not only did contradictions exist, but they were necessary in making things whole. Just look at some of Confucius' proverbs:

- *A man living without conflicts, as if he never lives at all.*
- *Life is really simple, but we insist on making it complicated.*
- *Real knowledge is to know the extent of one's ignorance.*

Opposites and how they interconnect were consistent themes. It was also generally believed that Confucius didn't actually say or write any of these proverbs, but still he's given credit. Maybe he would find this agreeable.

Think about the "Socrates is mortal" logic. Compare that to the Confucian idea that "A is right, but B is not wrong." Consider those two different starting points.

Teach one group of people Socrates' ideas and another group Confucius'. Separate them. Build a wall, start some religions, add in some war, and then, a few thousand years later, give everyone Skype and make them work together. This was the global system today and here we were, two business nomads, trying to navigate the differences.

What is truth? Depends where you are

Taoism, another Eastern philosophy/religion, came about roughly the same time as Confucianism, around 6th to 5th century BC. If Confucianism focused on social matters, like how a country or business or family should be run, then Taoism is about man's search for meaning. The yin-yang symbol is Tao, suggesting contrary forces are both complementary and interdependent in the world. It is composed of the same image with its opposite stuck together. The two parts need to be together for things to work. The dark needs the light; the light needs the dark.

As "Asia" was yin-ing and yanging, the Western world was heading in a different, linear direction, using logic as a baseline in studying individual subjects. Mathematics illustrates how these two mindsets viewed the worlds around them. The Greeks made massive inroads in the study of math, discovering, among other things, the Pythagorean theorem. You may not remember it, but most fifth-graders know that the square of the hypotenuse (the side opposite the right angle) is equal to the sum of the squares of the other two sides. Pythagoras discovered a system where geometric elements mapped to numbers, and where whole numbers and their ratios were all that was needed to build a logical system. Very Greek.

But things were about to get more complicated for the Greek number crunchers. Pythagoras had a student named Hippasus who proved that some calculations could not be expressed in fractions of whole numbers. These "irrational numbers" messed up the elegant mathematical world Pythagoras had promised. It was an attack on the system.[3]

What to do? Simple. Kill Hippasus. As the story goes, the unfortunate man was drowned, possibly by the Pythagoreans, after he started blabbing about his findings. Chinese mathematicians had their own quirks, but irrational numbers weren't one of them.

And this wasn't the only mathematical murder. The Greeks also disliked the number zero because, to them, zero wasn't a number. A number represented an amount. Zero represented nothing, a non-amount. Logic dictated it was not a number. Therefore, zero was a contradiction. It represented the value of nothing as a number even though nothing cannot be represented. Nothing is nothing, right? How did the Greeks handle this contradiction? Easy, they killed the mathematicians who tried to promote it. These were dangerous times to be a Greek numbers nerd.

The Chinese had no problem using zero. Who cared if it was illogical? It worked, use it. Yin and yang were happily hanging out with the math geeks. But ancient mathematics aside, what did this have to do with modern business problems? A lot, it turned out.

I was reminded of the many times Smitty had complained about his issues working in China. "Mate, I cannot tell you how often we have contract problems with our Chinese partners." His story echoed countless others. "They break, or altogether ignore, what we agreed to, and I have to go back to the bosses in Europe and the US and explain what's going on."

Chen was getting at the idea that things like contracts and agreements were perceived in fundamentally different ways depending on where someone come from. In fact, *truth* in the West was perceived as absolute. It either was or was not. But this was not the case in many of the fastest-growing markets in the world.

"Contracts and laws, the way you people think about them, don't make sense when things are constantly changing," Chen said. "Why would anyone lock themselves into a corner if they are trying to get things done? It closes out options." In other words, people looked at the same piece of paper and saw it as two very different things.

"Back at the end of 2001, you guys"—again he meant the West—"were focused on 9/11, but only a few weeks after that, China got into the World Trade Organization. My friend and I laughed and laughed because you Westerners actually thought China would stick to the agreement! It doesn't work that way. They stick to what makes sense for them. Truth is more flexible."[4]

Chen snapped an order to the waitress. "We will drink Taiwanese whisky and toast to *guanxi*." He kept pointing at the salt and mustard, "and I will explain *guanxi*."

"It starts with big things, like our surroundings and how we interact within it. But it's also about the group and how every person acts within that group." He was saying that each relationship was tied into a greater whole. The overall environment, the bigger things, took precedent over the smaller things. In this case, the individual.

I wanted to borrow Chen's coaster to keep writing, but by now his was in tiny pieces. Bigger to smaller. He hadn't done that to make a point though, he was high-strung and getting more tipsy.

Listening to and watching Chen reminded me of a quote from Geert Hofstede, the Dutch social psychologist Jake followed, who defined culture as "the collective programming of the mind which distinguishes the members of one group or category of people from another." It started to make sense why Chen was the way he was. Raised in Taiwan and educated in the United States, was this guy fighting two different types of mental programing?

Desperate for something to take notes on, I pulled out Chen's business card and starting writing on it, which seemed to prompt a flurry of new ideas from my new drinking buddy. Holding the mustard container, Chen went on, "We say someone's family name first, then their given name. The family is more important than the person." Bigger to smaller. I remembered the visa application to China and other countries in the region. For the date of birth, they ask in order of the year, then the month, then, finally, the day. Bigger to smaller.

The individual was not important in comparison to the greater group. In Chinese culture, the family took precedent over everything else. The big idea was that group dynamics took priority over the individual, and a focus on the larger whole sometimes resulted in different outcomes. It often meant not getting in the way. The cultural focus on *harmony* was a common theme across the region. Harmony was about being in balance with your surroundings. After all, everything was connected, so don't rock the boat. It was about agreement and respecting your family, specifically your parents. At a country level, it was about respecting your leaders and showing deference to your boss at work.

"You want to know why we give out business cards with both hands? It's because of *respect*. Respect of title, respect of name." He was right. The countless meetings where business cards were handed out, studied, and lined up in order of seniority seemed to an outsider like an odd corporate ritual, but now it started to make more sense. Job titles were much more important in these cultures compared to what I was used to back home. "Showing respect, by the way, meant never writing on someone's business card." I sank down in my seat, having committed yet another cultural faux pas. So I took his card and put it in my back pocket, which made Chen laugh even more. "Showing respect also means not putting my business card on your ass."

Name cards were no laughing matter. A $2 billion-dollar-a-year publishing company recently decided to standardize job titles across all their offices around the world. The decision came from their headquarters in the United States. They did it to simplify things. But across Asia, the results were disastrous. Some found their job title had been demoted. To make up for it, employees were paid a bit more, but in the Singapore and Hong Kong offices, this did not matter. To have one's title diminished was an insult money wouldn't fix. Key employees across the region up and left, taking their clients with them. This seemingly small change cost the company millions.

Competitors were more than happy to provide job titles of significance and purpose. This was no abstract concept; it's an important factor in understanding local markets.

Quiet

This cultural history lesson connected to other business challenges. "You gweilos complain we don't speak up in meetings," Chen said. By now we were several rounds of drinks deep. "We're not all shy! We're just being normal. We're working within the group. It's not right to speak up before we know everyone agrees. Or maybe we want to make the boss happy. When we hear you people talking nonstop, it sounds like everyone is showing off. Talking for the sake of talking." I thought of a million examples of conference calls where that was exactly the case. Thinking about all those annoying conference calls from this new perspective made them seem even more insane. Telling a foreign counterpart who was quiet to speak up on team calls was like saying, "Hey, you know how we all repeat the same stuff over and over so that it seems like we are all participating? You need to do that too."

Susan Cain spent a chapter of her bestselling book *Quiet: The Power of Introverts in a World That Can't Stop Talking* looking at the East/West cultural views toward speaking up. She wrote that statistically, Asian cultures were traditionally introverted while Western cultures were extroverted, and this seemed to affect how people across the world view leadership qualities. The West looked for leaders who stood out, spoke up, and made quick decisions, whereas preferred qualities on the other side of the planet included introspection and the importance of *what* was said rather than *how* it was said. Asians routinely found they hit a "bamboo ceiling," preventing them from promotions to leadership roles within Western organizations. Often, their lack of extroverted qualities was one of the reasons they were not promoted.

Staying quiet could also lead to expensive mistakes. One of the main reasons companies hired local talent was for their help in navigating the business through tricky local issues. But how does that work in places where speaking up was culturally shunned? Finding people who would speak up and who were assertive turned out to be one of the thorniest and most unexpected challenges of opening offices in many parts of the world.

Organizations would stumble around markets, asking for answers that many local hires were not culturally programed to give. Or worse, companies made decisions based on wrong answers their local employees *thought* their bosses wanted to hear.

Chen's comments had hit home. I thought about all the gripe sessions at the expat bars, complaining about how no one speaks their mind and how no one shares ideas. The barroom conclusion was that Singaporeans, Chinese, Indian, (fill in the blank) people were timid, or worse, duplicitous. I also heard complaints from people across Asia saying Americans were loud, pushy, self-promoting, duplicitous and rude. The stereotypes and negative generalizations flew across all parts of the globe, many times the exact same accusations. Were we all just misunderstanding each other's working styles? And in business, how much money was this costing companies?

Another example was employee training sessions. From new-hire orientation to facilitating workshops, audiences reacted differently to training approaches. Across Asia, trainers found themselves in front of groups of people who would silently stare at them the whole day. Interactive sessions, they were not. Trainers unfamiliar with these challenges not only found this exhausting, but even worse, little learning occured, and invitations to do more training events did not materialize. Organizations spent millions of dollars rolling out global training campaigns, often insisting every session be done the same way in the name of consistency. But this was another case where understanding local styles and adapting made the difference between success and failure.

Here, Chen was going back thousands of years and looking at

fundamental differences between Westerners and Eastern world views. When acknowledging these differences, sometimes it only took small adjustments to group discussions to make all the difference. In the case of training sessions, the answer was to divide the large group into small pieces. Bigger to smaller. A room of 20 people would stare at a facilitator in silence but five smaller groups of four people each almost always got discussions going. Decibel levels shot up as the smaller groups chatted away. All that needed to happen was to have each small group nominate someone to speak for them and present their findings. It was simple and it worked.

These flashes of clarity triggered new feelings of hope. The business world didn't need to make everyone extroverted; it needed to figure out how to adjust to these different styles. This new Confucian insight filled me with a renewed energy and new ideas to try out with my team.

The world is hierarchical

The different views of relationships were closely tied to the idea of hierarchies, the social construct Axel and Jake obsessed over. Now I was finally beginning to understand why. "Silly Western companies who are so proud of their 'flat' business structures where everyone is treated equally. Wrong! That won't work with most of the people on the planet!" Even though Chen was laughing at the saltshaker, this was an important topic and one where opinions varied widely.

A Scandinavian company selling advanced project management solutions had recently high-tailed it out of Malaysia because local employees kept quitting due to a "lack of leadership." Stephan, the general manager for APAC, was beside himself trying to figure out what to do. Employees kept complaining, so he kept giving them more freedom and leeway to do what they wanted. "I wanted them to feel comfortable with me! I wanted them to call me by my first name and feel free to consider me just another part of the team." He wanted to adjust and figure out how to make the company's project management programs work for local audiences, and he expected his team to bring him the ideas to get it done. Perhaps he had approached it all wrong. Maybe he was not treating people the way they want to be treated.

Flat hierarchies were also wreaking havoc within companies introducing "agile" team models. The agile approach essentially meant that a team was created based on specific skill sets needed for a specific project. Teams were fast, lean, and focused on delivery without the layers of unnecessary management. This was a great idea, but one based on the assumption that each team member communicated clearly with one another, regardless of rank. Time and time again companies wrestled with figuring out why some members refused to speak up, and frequently cultural differences, like how people behaved in flat versus vertical hierarchies, were the culprit.

We kept talking about Confucius, so I asked, did Confucius one day show up and start laying down a hierarchal collectivist society in pursuit of harmony? With the same flair he had shown all night, Chen responded, "Nah, we were into rice way before Confucius was around."

I liked this guy. Now, apparently, we were talking about rice. "Rice farming is communal. It must be. You need to work with everyone else who's growing rice near you because of the irrigation and complexities of growing this stuff," he said, shaking the mustard container.

Anthropologists have been studying this topic for decades. By looking at regional differences in agricultural trends, a picture had developed of societies, and even cultures, evolving out of how people grew their food. This was anthropology, sociology, geography, and economics rolled into two condiments and local whisky. Confucius didn't change his society; he just summarized it.

Growing wheat, it was argued, was a lot easier than growing rice. You didn't need as many people, and farmers working next to each other weren't as tied into a collective need to work together and grow their crops in the exact same way as their neighbors.

I thought about my call center, my problems, Confucius and

rice farming, and the number zero that the Greeks didn't accept as a number. I thought about logic and all the times I had heard Western expats complain that people in the region "couldn't think logically," and locals across the region wondering why Westerners were so focused on specific agreements and doing things "their way." Was this where these misunderstandings originated?

"Now, I'm only scratching the surface and talking about things that are easy to explain. Do you still think that Western businesspeople understand our ideas around relationships?"

My new Taiwanese friend had handed me 5,000 years of history using a plastic mustard bottle and a saltshaker. It wasn't just about speaking up. Heatmap tests showed people from different parts of the world looked at websites differently. Westerners tended to look at one area at a time. Chinese take in the entire page at once. Bigger to smaller. Smart ecommerce companies adjusted their page layouts accordingly. Dating apps that worked in one part of the world would fail to take off elsewhere. In Hong Kong, a local company built a dating app based on the assumption that people didn't go on first dates with a stranger alone, they did it in groups. There were different cultural patterns at play here that impacted products and services.

"With all of these differences, was it even possible for companies to localize around the globe effectively?" I asked Chen. He gave me a friendly but slightly condescending smile. "That's a very Western way of thinking about it."

Chen had given me new ideas for understanding, explaining and adjusting to different cultural situations. The history of regions clearly affected how cultures evolved, and this helped better explain the working style differences we all wrestle with. It was one thing to change your working style when going to another part of the world; it was another thing to understand *why*. Whether on a conference call with a client in Dubai or managing a remote team in India or getting into a contract negotiation with a Chinese partner, I had picked up all kinds of tricks and tools for handling tough international situations.

I was building a *Global Survival Kit*.

Survival Guide Tips:

✔ To increase participation within global teams, create smaller groups in conference calls, meetings and training sessions. *Bigger to Smaller.*

✔ Global leaders in business need to be thoughtful not just vocal. Introverted teammates are the most underutilized assets in many organizations. Find and nurture them.

Chapter 8

Future Skills

"Key skills of tomorrow don't yet exist. Show me someone who gets excited by this notion and I'll show you someone who is future proof."

—*Diana David Wu*

The talented people needed to navigate today's volatile business world were in front of us the whole time. Here is how my company found great people—and how they found creative and unusual ways to solve emerging market challenges.

I N 2008, it seemed as if the world stopped.

While sitting at a bar overlooking the Singapore Strait, I looked up only to notice that the cargo ships had stopped moving. What normally would have been a series of enormous marine vessels floating freely along an oceanic superhighway had quickly turned into a highly congested traffic jam rivaling any megacity's worst rush hour.

Singapore was one of the world's busiest port cities, hosting roughly 2,000 ships per day and serving as an epicenter of global trade. Suddenly, no one was buying anything. Ships filled with fuel, toys, cars, clothes, food, electronics, and god knows what else, bobbed in the warm, oily, equatorial waters. It seemed the only things more congested than the strait were the downtown bars. Our local was filled with shipping traders by noon. It was standing room only by 2 p.m. These guys had nothing to trade except rumors and speculation as to what might happen next.

The irony of an economic downturn was that businesses like mine could capitalize on them—when employees got laid off, those same companies then must outsource more work. People were getting laid off by the thousands stateside and in Europe, but business opportunities in Asia seemed to be multiplying, making this an especially opportune moment to try something bold. In the case of 2008–09, Western companies that weren't finding growth opportunities at home had quickly shifted their focus to Asia. Companies of all shapes and sizes saw Asia as the only way to continue to feed their growth addiction.

Unfortunately, I had still not figured out how to find a team of sales hunters, but an aha moment that inspired me to rethink talent acquisition was about to take place. Like so many breakthroughs, it happened by accident.

As I sat in the bar looking at the ships, I got a call from Texas Joe, who had received yet *another* pathetic campaign update from my team.

"Hey, Joe." My voice trembled.

"Son, can you explain what in the hell your people are doing over there?"

I was asking myself the same question. How could I justify this?

"Joe, I just saw these numbers myself, and they're lower than they need to be."

No shit.

"No shit," he said.

I found courage. I got defensive. After all, this guy didn't get it. He didn't understand how different things were over here. This *slap dragon*. Claire was having the same problem, and he knew it. I took a breath and told him about esses and sees. I talked about cultural differences and the importance of doing research and building relationships and how this takes time and that is why we were making fewer dials. After all, this was about Confucius. Joe was *lucky* to have me explain how things really were. How circular everything was depending on the culture you grew up in. You know, yin and yang, and...rice farmers.

I stopped and waited for Joe's response. He had rehired me to help him build a sales pipeline, and instead I had given him a barrage of excuses where I blamed Confucius and ancient agrarian farming techniques.

"Suhn," he said as he inhaled air at the same time he spoke. I cringed.

"I don't give a *fiddler's fuck* about esses and sees and con-fusin' rice, and whatever you're talking about. We are done."

And there it was. I had been fired by Texas Joe...again.

I ordered a beer and stared off toward the sea as the bartender told me it is one-for-one. "No problem," I replied mindlessly, "first one now and the second one later."

Two seats away a woman who had been eavesdropping said, "Another foreigner with employee problems. That's unique."

Sarcasm. Rare in these parts. Who was this person? She was well dressed and looked to be in her late 40s.

"It's very hard to find good talent here," she said as she moved, uninvited, to the stool next to mine. "It's not exactly Singapore's. It's a tiny place. Lots of demand," she smiled into her drink, "Lots."

This was starting to sound like either a business lesson or pick-up line. Maybe both.

"I need salespeople," I said, deciding to make her my temporary therapist. "People who aren't afraid to pick up the phones and talk to strangers. People who don't care if they get rejected most of the time. I can't seem to find them here."

"Import them."

"I can't afford it. I'd have to massively raise my prices, and this region seems to be really price sensitive." The irony of drinking 15-dollar beers did not escape me.

"Then don't pay your people."

Smiling, I played along. "Sure, I'll just…not pay them," I said, throwing some sarcasm back at her. I realized I missed sarcasm. The feeling of homesickness hit during little moments like these.

She introduced herself as Ms. Lin and told me her story. Part of her story, at least.

Ms. Lin also had a people problem. She solved it by traveling around Southeast Asia and bringing talent to work for her in Singapore. Since most of the region was considerably less wealthy than this mega-rich city-state, working here was considered a golden ticket—an opportunity most people would be crazy to pass up. One worth making short-term sacrifices for.

She told me about her hiring process. She knew what she was looking for, which was half the battle. She found employees and paid for them to move to Singapore. She handled the employment paperwork and took care of housing. But she didn't pay her employees. At least not right away. They had to work their way into a revenue-sharing agreement.

She had my full attention as she continued.

For the first two weeks, a new employee had to work for Ms. Lin and bring in as much business as possible. There was a target number and if that number wasn't hit, the employee was sent home. Here was the brutal part: Ms. Lin didn't tell the new hires how much money they needed to make during those first two weeks for them to stay. As soon as many workers hit targets they tended to slow down, so she made the sales targets invisible.

Hunters kept hunting.

For those who made the cut after the first two weeks, metrics were provided and a tiered commission plan established. At first, Ms. Lin would take in most of the profits, but over time, the employees began to earn more and more.

"Then I want them out," she declared. "If they are that good, they won't stay with me for more than two years, at most. I encourage them to leave and start their own business. That's how I got started."

This was an aggressive system, but fitting based on the kind of hunters I needed in my sales teams. I paused. Was I talking to a competitor? What exactly was Ms. Lin selling?

"I run the spas and karaoke bars in this part of town. Let me know if you want to meet some of my girls? I'll give you a first-timer's discount. You look like a first-timer." She winked.

Not a competitor. And how awful. Ms. Lin's prostitution ring was not going to help me, and besides, the people I needed weren't going to work for free, end of story. I closed my bar bill and ended the conversation.

Wait a minute. My instincts had let me down when interpreting overseas work situations. Axel and others had cautioned me about this. *Ignore your instincts for a moment.* I looked at the ships. The unmoving ships. I thought about unpaid, imported karaoke bar workers. On the other side of the planet, the financial crisis had decimated the job market. The people I was looking for were now either out of a job or graduating with few career options. Like the ships, Wall Street had come to a standstill. Who goes to Wall Street to make a ton of money selling stuff? Dominant personality types—D-types. There were a lot of newly impoverished salespeople loitering around the States. People with the exact skill sets I wanted.

Using behavioral profiling models, I knew the kind of person I was looking for. The Global Financial Crisis created this pool of underutilized talent. They just happened to be on the other side of the world. If I took the mama-san's advice, I might just have a model to do it.

I threw together a job description for the kind of person I wanted. Along with being dominant, they needed to be social, friendly, and able to adapt quickly and pick up new skills. After all, I was going to fly people from the other side of the planet, put them into a foreign culture, and get them to sell stuff to hundreds of people every month from over a half dozen countries they've probably never been to. They had to learn fast and adjust in real time.

I needed liberal arts majors.

Having graduated from a small liberal arts school in Maine called Bowdoin College, I reached out to their career development team. Within a matter of days, I had a stack of résumés.

Cult of personality

Soon after, Mikey J. stood outside my door. He looked like someone who had just moored his sailboat off Martha's Vineyard and was heading out to a lobster bake. His appearance was the epitome of a New England Yankee. A blue blood to the bone. Were those pink whales on a blue belt holding up a pair of Nantucket reds? This guy was a larger-than-life personality, but he had a secret. He was broke. Not just broke but living off welfare checks as a teenager before earning a full scholarship to Bowdoin. His background gave him an aura of intensity and a drive most preppy New Englanders didn't possess. The outfit was purely for show. This guy was a survivor.

An "emancipated minor," Mikey essentially divorced himself from his parents when he was 17 years old. He grew up in poverty between Cape Cod and Maine with abusive and drug-addicted parents.[1] He had half-siblings scattered around New England. His immediate family tree looked more like a ragged thorn bush.

The fact that he was damaged goods was what made him so formidable. This kid knew adversity firsthand and he had proven himself a fighter.

This was a risky plan because Mike had no money and no other options, but I had no better ideas. We were ready to begin this experiment—until swine flu.

To understand why countries take virus outbreaks like the 2008 swine flu and 2019 novel coronavirus so seriously, it's helpful to understand SARS. As those working across Southeast Asia over the past few decades will attest, the SARS epidemic had more of an impact on their psyche than the more frequently cited east Asian financial crisis of 1997.[2]

Back in 2002, when SARS was moving from a simmer to a boil, Singapore went into a science-fiction-like lockdown. People couldn't enter buildings without having a temperature check from an attendant in a full hazmat suit. Some offices were outfitted with plastic sheeting that separated rooms. Files got passed between specially built windows as if people were handling radiation. Millions of people were suddenly living inside sterilized bubbles. It has been estimated that the cost of SARS worldwide was over $50 billion dollars.[3]

The coronavirus resulted in mandatory quarantines for anyone flying in from infected regions. The swine flu quarantine was not as severe but Mikey's new landlady took no chances and would not let him into her apartment for seven days, the government-recommended quarantine period. This meant I had a new 22-year-old roommate.[4]

There was nothing else to do but give him breakfast and take him to the office and throw him on the phones. "I thought I was supposed to be quarantined?" he asked as we got on the crowded subway.

Appetite for creative destruction

Mikey was given the tough accounts, even with little training. He was the guy who figured things out quickly. Once, after being rejected by a series of failed cold calls, he looked out the window and said, "Those guys I just called...they're all located downtown. I should just go down there and explain this stuff to them, so they understand." And with that he was off. Cold calling could only get you so far. "Everyone here says you can't do business over the phone, so to hell with it, I'll show up at their office. Dude, can I borrow a dollar for the train?"

I had finally found my hunter. No one, and I mean no one, saw Mikey J coming. He was a sales generation animal without fear or remorse. Sure, he'd let someone say no, but they sure as hell must have a good reason why. In cultures that stress harmony, Mike was pure pandemonium.

He embraced the Ghostbuster Principle in all its forms. We were asked if we could build a massive database in Korean language, a feat we did not have the language skills to perform. Mikey begged me to bid on it. When we won the contract, I looked at him. "How the hell are we going to do this?"

"I'll get it done."

On time, he delivered as promised. "I know some Korean girls who took it as extra work. They're students and were glad to earn the cash." Mikey pocketed a healthy commission.

A few months after that, Mikey realized he had made a mistake.

He had sent the database back to the client with a passcode, which was common. A list of names and email addresses on a simple spreadsheet was worth millions in the right hands. Documents like these were easy to copy, replicate, and send around, so keeping them protected was a top priority. That's why the least we could do was put a password on the completed projects.

But Mikey had sent the client the wrong password, preventing them from opening and using the data...three months ago.

The client in question had never mentioned the wrong code, which meant only one thing. The database had never been opened. I double checked. This was a $40,000 project where a small army of Korean speakers spent hundreds—if not thousands—of hours building contacts. There was information on this database that could translate into millions of dollars of new business. But no one had tried to open it.

This was not unheard of. Large companies that grew around the globe at breathtaking speeds had projects that fell through the cracks, but in the rush to expand, these cracks had become tectonic in size. It was common for a new team out of, say, Korea, or China, or ASEAN to report to a manager based in the United States, Australia or the UK who would have these massive geographies added to their already heavy workload. With speed and distance came mistakes.

So long as everyone was focused on growth, growth, growth, no one seemed to notice things like an unopened $40,000 marketing project. When we called the client to let her know about the wrong password, we were told she had left the company and there was no one currently handling her role. The database remained unopened.

And we were a small agency. The larger firms were experiencing the same thing only with more zeros at the end of each project value. A few million dollars would get allocated to a "high-potential" market somewhere and vanish.

There was an undeniable trend forming with clients rushing into new regions, throwing money around but with no clear purpose other than making quick wins. Was anyone overseeing what was going on?

We were more than happy to go along for the ride and Mikey was just as wild as these companies, which made him a perfect fit.

Another thing happened: the small projects got bigger. Mikey body-slammed them to completion, asking for more. To describe him in a word, *profitable*. Two words, *very profitable*. Other unpaid hires came onboard and were equally successful, earning commissions and spending those commissions, having a blast along the way.

Social media platforms spread their stories back in the United States, and their readership increased as each crazy Asian tale got weirder and weirder.

The chatter eventually made it to a journalist, and a major news outlet published an article about interns who overcame the recession. This landed us unintentional but helpful PR. Our "internship" became a lead story and that quickly went viral. The internet gods had decided we had the best internship program in the world.

Because of the social media attention, résumés flooded in not only from college grads but from business school grads. The timing could not have been better. Mikey's three-month contract with me was coming to an end. However, I had an unusual project that he was perfect for, which will be explained shortly. So he got to stick around a bit longer.

There were many hundreds more Mikeys wanting to join. The one-way trip from the United States to Singapore kicked into high gear as the office filled up with ambitious foreigners, many of whom never thought about working overseas but were now happy to work for free in order to get a foot in the door of Asia. I suddenly had an army of accidental business nomads.

This created a problem. I needed to figure out how to get them out once their three-month stint ended. The answer also happened by accident. One of our client's sales managers from a large tech firm visited our office.

"Where did you find *these people*?" he asked. An American expat, he was pulling his hair out, struggling with the same problems that Claire the Bulldog and I had been working through. Where was the local talent that was willing to chew shards of glass and ask for more? Where were the hunters? He didn't know how to articulate it, but he had the same *esses and sees* problem.

"Can I have one?" he jokingly asked. "You can, for a price," was my response. And somewhere during that four seconds of sarcastic banter we realized we had found a solution to both of our problems. I needed to help these great hunters find career paths and get them out of my office because I had what seemed like a limitless supply of near-free labor waiting in the wings. The sales manager needed full-time talent and had a budget to pay salaries. Thus began a wonderful global sales talent ecosystem. He hired my company for consulting work. Our callers worked full-time on his sales team. The monthly fee covered a reasonable starting salary while paying my company for finding, vetting, and training his new employees. Why couldn't companies do this themselves? Changing systems was hard, especially when decision making was fragmented or happening 10,000 miles away at a headquarters unfamiliar with local challenges.

Companies loved the idea and we brought over more people. Best of all the salespeople loved it because they had clear entry points into some of the fastest-growing technology companies in the fastest-growing markets in the world.

Over the next two years, we hired talented people from all over the world.

We mastered the art of identifying sales skill sets that companies needed. Not skill sets they *thought* they needed, but *really* needed. Number one on the list was adaptability. How quickly could someone assess a situation and change behavior? Could they be creative, and did they have the guts to try new ideas even if they failed?

Ironically this was exactly the opposite of how most companies hired people. Over and over again, job descriptions insisted on graduates from the top universities with top scores. This was especially the case in parts of the world where hierarchies were strong. Everyone was looking for top scores. Diverse résumés were ignored. And this was an opportunity for companies willing to think differently. Here is how we cracked the code of finding local talent.

Flipping the stack

While foreign interns kept flooding into our office, I had by no means given up on finding local talent. I partnered with a local university to send us students, but the first few interns they sent did not work out. They were all the top of their class, but everyone seemed unwilling, or unable, to improvise. No one had ever asked them to do what we were asking—to learn about a new product, call a bunch of strangers, and ask them a bunch of questions. Would they adapt? It was not happening. My team was about to end the relationship with the school when they sent us a woman by accident. They didn't mean to send her because she was one of their *worst* students. But Uma was exactly who we were looking for.

Of Malaysian descent, we learned that Uma was a bad student because she was disruptive in class. This meant that she asked a lot of questions and challenged teachers. This was a good sign. She had also been told she was not good enough to succeed in a corporate job because she hadn't learned the skills that other students had aced. Uma understood rejection because people had been rejecting her all her life. In a rigid education system obsessed with standardized testing, someone like Uma got quickly moved aside. As sad as her story was, we had found our local rockstar. The lesson here was clear: The skills we wanted—adaptability and creativity and being unafraid of failing—were hiding in plain sight in many parts of the world. Better yet, they were being ignored by other companies.

Hiring teams often organized graduate résumés in order of grade point average, from highest to lowest. Today, when I consult with these companies, I take the stack of résumés and flip them over and start from the bottom. We should be looking first at those who "failed" based on measurements from the past. Agility, learning from failure and adaptability are the skills for the future.

Clients brought us new challenges all the time, forcing us to get creative. Dozens of languages were spoken across the region, and this was an obstacle. In one situation, I was both impressed by our ingenuity and caught off guard by my preconceived biases.

A client asked if we could translate their marketing material into Thai. And they asked if could we complete it in three days (their current translation company said it would take two weeks). Our Ghostbusters, cowboy culture was in high-gear and, of course, we said yes. We didn't provide translation services, nor did we have a Thai speaker on staff. But the ambitious hunters in the room were eager to get creative and figure it out.

Everyone went into the conference room. Dodging internet cables and mismatched chairs, the team started throwing ideas around.

This was before the days of freelancing websites, where you could find these skills online. *Does anyone know any Thai speakers? What if we call the Thai embassy? What about Craigslist? How much would it cost to fly to Bangkok?* Something more immediate was needed. *What about Orchard Towers?* Came a suggestion from one intern. The room giggled because Orchard Towers was stacked with bars of ill repute.

"No, seriously, what if we went to the bars where there are a bunch of Thai women and asked them? Maybe one of them has a sister or brother who could help us."

This was a bad idea, but it was the best we had. We gave the guy $50 for "market research" and sent him off. "Should I bring back receipts?"

"No!"

Within a few hours, our fearless employee called. "I've got it all sorted out, don't worry about it. Also, I'm not coming back to the office today, something's come up."

Uh huh.

Whatever came up on his end didn't matter, because our translation problem was solved. A woman working at one of the bars who said she used to be an English teacher back in her hometown outside of Bangkok agreed to do the translation during the day before her other work began. Within a day, we received a fully translated document and sent it to the client hoping it got accepted.

Not only did they accept it, they loved it. The client's managing director from Thailand thought it was great and asked if we would handle all their translation work. This was a big opportunity. I said yes immediately.

Now I had to find the woman and see if she wanted a full-time job. I assumed she'd take the offer. After all, this was an opportunity to escape from sex work. She was getting a chance for better and safer opportunities. I admit I thought I was a hero who found a capitalistic solution to at least one person's social problems.

But she turned me down.

It turned out she was not interested in being "saved." Most important, I couldn't match the money she was making. To her, this offer was a bad career move. The corporate world was untrustworthy and risky, and she preferred her current situation. This interaction blindsided me. I was guilty of making assumptions. Assumptions about prostitution, assumptions about education levels, and skill sets. Once again, what I thought I knew turned out to be wrong.

Without our rockstar Thai translator, we couldn't build the translation business, at least in any reasonable manner. Having unpaid interns lurking around Orchard Towers soliciting prostitutes for corporate jobs was not feasible. We got lucky once, so it was best not to push it. Thus ended our translation adventure.

It wasn't only language issues that required creative problem solving. Clients desperate to find new markets to sell their products ventured into smaller cities across Asia. This was often a waste of time because these small cities really did not have much need for high-end IT products. But we ended up building a lot of lists because the pressure was on for our clients to show growth.

If growing into emerging markets was the gold rush of this era, then we were the ones selling shovels to those rushing in to make a quick buck. In this case our shovels took the form of databases filled with small companies, most of whom were not at all interested in buying our client's expensive tech products.

How to find small companies and contacts scattered across Southeast Asia? As far as we knew, the data didn't exist, so we had to get creative. Mikey J was the man for the job.

Cities included: Da Nang in Vietnam, Las Piñas in the Philippines, Shah Alam in Malaysia, and an island in Indonesia called Bunaken.

"Isn't Bunaken an island for divers? Don't they run on generators? What do tech companies want with that kind of database?" Mikey already spotted the fatal flaw of this project. No one in these small towns and cities was going to buy our clients' stuff.

But our clients didn't want to hear the feedback. We agreed to do it.

His assignment: build a database of 50,000 contacts of people in cities and islands he had mostly never heard of across five countries. We were getting paid more than $100,000 to get this done. I offered Mikey $15,000 and asked him to deliver the database in 60 days. "I don't care how, just keep it legal and don't tell me any details."

"I'm in. I'll do it."

Think about that assignment. A broke 23-year-old gets given $15,000 dollars and an adventure across Asia. There was no supervision, and he could do whatever he wanted wherever he wanted. It was a dream come true, especially in the dark days after the global financial crisis. If he could somehow find an existing database, he could spend the next two months drinking cocktails on the beaches of Thailand living like a king. Maybe it was that easy, maybe much harder. No one knew.

"I'm all over this. And, uh, when you say 'legal,' what do you mean?"

"I mean I don't want to know what you do to get this done." This last statement summed up many businesses' overseas strategies.

So off went Mikey J into the steamy underbelly of Southeast Asia in search for a giant database of contacts who would never consider buying high-end IT hardware. In the next chapter, we'll dig into how Mike got his data and what we did with it.

The mama-san-inspired business plan turned out to be a complicated case study. On one hand, flying in talent from around the world solved the problem of finding sales hunters. It was a creative and profitable solution. On the other hand, the business was essentially designed to bring Westerners into Asia and fill our Western clients' offices with more Westerners. This was not exactly the right way to win over local markets.

During this rapid hiring phase, I accidentally found local talent as well. Companies were looking for top graduates and academic superstars, but the skill sets of adaptability, resilience and curiosity did not seem to be correlated to high grades, especially in parts of the world where education was more rigid and structured. These creative people thrived in uncertainty. And they were a little crazy, which certainly helped.

Survival Guide Tips:

- ✔ To find and retain talent, organizations have to rethink hiring and training. The skills of the future include adaptability, creativity and resiliency. These traits exist today, but you have to look beyond traditional hiring practices to find them. *Flip the Stack.*

- ✔ When making decisions don't trust your gut. Instincts are based on familiar, not unfamiliar, settings. Gut instincts in international, unfamiliar, situations can be a liability. Pause before making important decisions.

Chapter 9

Chasing the
White Rabbit

"We're all mad here."

—The Cheshire Cat from Alice in Wonderland

This is the story of my big break and how it nearly broke me. Working globally means partnering locally. Finding partners and making those relationships work well is hard and requires adaptability, but many organizations and people are not set up for this. This story illustrates the challenge and lessons from an ambitious project designed to apply global standards to local realities.

PARTNERING WITH local companies has become more important today than ever because local markets want local solutions. Partners on the ground are the best way to do this. Partnering can be a fast path to quick growth. However, making these relationships work has never been easy. From the call center in Cebu, I had already seen what happens when companies come into new regions sticking to their old scripts. Things got ugly and expensive, fast.

The following is a story of another, more outrageous clash between a giant multinational corporation and how they tried to standardize their partners across the globe in a desperate quest to bring in business. Like the other examples throughout these pages, the names have been changed to protect the guilty. What was funny was how often this sort of thing happend in large organizations. What was tragic about it was how it happened over and over again, and no one seemed to learn from the mistakes. It was my big opportunity, my chance to massively expand across Asia and then the world. And this is how and why several of us caused the entire project to collapse.

The sales target that must never be questioned

This story begins with a revenue target, a Number. The Number, never to be questioned, instructed sales teams at publicly traded companies how much they needed to sell for the quarter and the year. No one knew how this Number was derived. No one could ask. This was not an exaggeration: in this particular tech company, it was forbidden to ask where the Number came from. Was it based on last year's Number and increased by 5% to 20%? Maybe. The fact that the Number from the previous year was missed by half, or more, was irrelevant. Pointing out this kind of thing was career suicide.

We referred to this client as *the mothership,* and everyone within its gravitational pull was terrified of their Number.

Remember, this was happening during the crazy emerging market boom at the beginning of the twenty-first century. So the Number rolling down the chain of command, for this company and others, was especially bold. Emerging markets were looked at as the saviors that would miraculously cover for everyone else's revenue shortcomings. The Number landed on the laptops of the dozens or hundreds of vice presidents who passed it down to their senior directors, whose eyes would bulge as they passed the audacious figure down to their directors. They would toss it to the managers, who sprinkled it across regions. No questions. Just make it happen.

Mr. Axel referred to the Number as a "white rabbit."

"Run—don't walk—away from this," he told me one day. "They pull this number out of the sky. This…this rabbit. They pull a rabbit out of the clouds! They make it your problem. Everyone is chasing this cloudy white rabbit." His mixed metaphor may have had something to do with his long day out with the Centurions, but regardless, this was not the advice I wanted to hear. I had just won a giant regional pilot project that, if all went well, would turn into a worldwide account worth tens of millions of dollars. It was my chance to build a global marketing powerhouse supporting the biggest companies currently leading the hyper-globalization charge. Sure, the sales targets were ludicrous, but I was focused on three letters: MDF.

Market Development Funds contained a lot of money. These programs invested in marketing campaigns for business partners. Business partners in the world of large tech companies were local businesses that resold the larger companies products. There were tens of thousands of business partners that sold the mothership's products, which meant there were tens of thousands of funded projects around the world for agencies like mine to win. We had been hired to take the money and use it to build sales pipelines for each and every partner.

Assume for a moment that a partner starts selling the mothership's products. What happens is that a percentage of each sale is carved out and put back into this market development fund. The idea was to constantly reinvest in marketing efforts to build new business. For a marketing agency like mine, it was a perpetual money machine.

If a hundred business partners each sold $1 million worth of products, MDF took, say, 10% of this and reinvested it for additional marketing efforts. That was now $100,000 per partner times a hundred partners, which equalled $10 million.

If this happened across 50 countries, that's *$100 million* in MDF.

And these are the *smaller* business partners. The larger strategic partners played with a lot more money.

There were hundreds of large companies across many industries each doing similar programs. Companies like mine were therefore quick to ignore market realities and pledge allegiance to something as outlandish as the Number.

As partner programs grew and expanded into new geographies, they became harder to manage. In many cases, partners were simply given the funds and told to use the money to bring in more sales. Accountability was scarce. There were a lot of MDF-sponsored Rolex watches ticking away, for example, and this was not the intent of the programs.

The mothership was one such giant company that had decided their global partner program had gotten out of control. They decided to take all the money back and give it to one agency to invest it responsibly. In theory, this approach was cheaper, faster and more accountable. There was now going to be one throat to choke if anything went wrong.

In this case, my company won the pilot program, where we took the MDF for 120 business partners. The throat in question, was going to be mine.

The 120 business partners in ASEAN were spread out across seven countries—Singapore, Malaysia, Thailand, Vietnam, Indonesia, Cambodia, and the Philippines. The year before, they were each given $10,000 directly and asked to report back with their progress. It worked out well for Rolex, but not the mothership. That was about to change.

How to run marketing campaigns for 120 business partners across multiple languages and geographies simultaneously while reporting progress to the mothership? We needed to standardize things as much as possible. Every business partner needed to have the same options in order to report and measure progress consistently. This was a problem because standardizing marketing campaigns across such a diverse region was fraught with issues. What worked in one city, such as a telemarketing effort, might fail elsewhere where cold calls weren't typical. Some places focused on face-to-face events where others wanted to run campaigns on social media platforms. But while Facebook might be popular in the Philippines, Twitter had more penetration in Indonesia. Every market was different so a blanket approach over the region was going to be hit or miss. I tried to push back but based on the way the program was set up, the only option was to standardize or walk away from the whole thing.

My team tried to create as many locally relevant ideas as possible, but the reality was that local and regional differences took a backseat in the name of standardization. *It worked in the United States, so it will work here.* This was what the mothership, with decades of experience across these regions, insisted upon. They were fixated on the Number, and the way to get there was to standardize. The millions of dollars of MDF were likely clouding my judgment because at the time, I thought it would work.

When global standardization meets local reality

As soon as we won the deal, surprises came fast and furiously. First, we learned that none of the business partners knew what was happening. We had to call and tell them. *You know that $10,000 dollars you were given last year with no real preconditions? We have it now and we are going to do some campaigns for you.*

How hard would it be to convince business partners to agree to work with us? It turned out, very hard.

Then we met the Mad Hatter.

Assigned as our day-to-day contact from the mothership, the Mad Hatter was an intense Malaysian national addicted to spreadsheets. She was singularly focused on data. Nothing else seems to matter. She did not appear to understand, or care about, the basics of sales and marketing, but she knew Excel inside out. This combination made her dangerous.

The most painful example came from the year before, when partners were asked to sell a product valued at around $25,000 apiece. However, a $25,000 price point would no longer work in her Excel formula in order to hit the new enormous Number. Her answer was to simply update the spreadsheet by doubling the anticipated product value to $50,000 dollars. This meant partners would be expected to sell new, more expensive products regardless of market demand. *I know you are looking to buy a bicycle, but you should really consider this BMW.* The product was switched to a more expensive version only because it made the spreadsheet work. No one seemed to think this was a problem. We named her the Mad Hatter based on her unabashed comfort with absurdity.

And she was just getting started. When bidding on the project, we were told the mothership would pay us an advance of around $350,000 dollars to help us get the team up and running. The Mad Hatter told us matter of factly that since Asian markets were growing so fast, we wouldn't need the money to get started. She seemed to have no issue with this argument, even though it made no sense. What was happening, in reality, was that the mothership was quietly cutting back on their spending. The higher-ups knew the Number was never getting hit, so they could at least help their bottom line by cutting costs. The Mad Hatter accepted these instructions from nameless higher-ups without question and kept plugging away at her spreadsheets.

For us, it meant getting paid many months later than expected.

To cover the initial costs, I put my entire life savings into the company bank account. It didn't cover what we needed, but it was a start. I believed we could get this done.

The team grew fast over a period of only a few weeks. We hired people in all seven countries. I was on autopilot trying to hire and train people as fast as possible. In retrospect, I had ignored many of the things I had learned from Jake the Snake, Claire, Axel and Chen. Ideas like slowing down and adjusting to local styles, getting to know new teammates and learning about their working styles were afterthoughts because the team was so understaffed and under tremendous pressure simply to keep up.

At the same time, the Mad Hatter made more changes to the program. Business partners could now split up how they spent their $10,000. They could do up to four smaller campaigns throughout the year. We now needed to get each partner to sign on to potentially four campaigns, rather than one. A partner, for example, could now choose to spend $3,000 on a calling campaign, then $2,000 on an email campaign a few months later, and then $2,500 each on two events later in the year. Things were moving so fast I didn't take the time to process the fact that this would be four times the amount of work for us. I was caught up in the growth and the money, just like everybody else. Stress quickly replaced the initial excitement of winning this project, and I fell into a mode where I was not thinking, only responding to problems. For example, my typical response to a new issue was to think about how I had handled similar problems back in the United States. I was ignoring everything I had learned about working in diverse markets. This was common when taking on overseas projects. Under stress, there is a tendency to develop tunnel vision and fall back on past behaviors in order to get them through tough situations.

I should have walked away from this project on many occasions. The payment terms were strangling our bank account. It was no longer 120 campaigns, it was four times that with horrible payment terms. In retrospect, it was clear how doomed this project was, but each change that made our lives more difficult was masked by that unmistakeable siren call of Market Development Funds and winning the larger global prize. After all, we were growing, so it was worth it, right?

There was another regional difference happening here as well. In the United States there was an unspoken agreement between the business partners, the marketing people, and the marketing agency that the Number was pure fiction. It was understood that the system was flawed and targets too high, and, therefore, the only way to keep everything from imploding was to help each other out. Everyone knew that if they told the mothership what they wanted to hear, everyone would be left alone. But on the other side of the planet, the rules, both spoken and unspoken, were different. The targets were more aggressive, and the game was being played by people who did not want to play along.

We were selling products that were twice as expensive as before into cities half the size of the usual markets. This, you may recall, was because partners were failing to hit the Number when selling into large cities across the region, so the mothership decided to go after smaller markets. How and why would tiny markets buy twice as much tech? We were not allowed to ask.

And speaking of those smaller cities, this is why Mikey J was sent off to Thailand to build that giant database. To make these campaigns successful, we needed data on 50,000 companies. We couldn't do any of the hundreds of business partner campaigns we had promised without a massive database of prospects to call into, so the data was critical.

Innovation is not always HR-approved

Unsurprisingly, Mikey was having the time of his life figuring out how to find information on 50,000 companies. He had wisely decided to start out in a few cities that happened to be located on, or near, amazing beaches. Chatting up surfer girls in Koh Samet, Thailand, he was introduced to women who worked at the equivalent of a Chamber of Commerce. Few people spoke English, but that wasn't going to stop Mikey.

Realizing that local government agencies were filled with twenty-something women who were willing to humor him, Mikey developed a plan.

This plan would not meet most HR codes of conduct. Details have never been provided, but photos he emailed of what he was up to spoke a thousand words, most of them scandalous. Our male-dominated office was envious. A new email from Mikey would arrive and the office would erupt in cheers, with papers and leftover food containers tossed into the air in celebration. He had become a legend.

As the bills come in and my cash went out, the first batch of data from Mikey arrived.

"Here's 3,000 records. This is awesome." At least someone was having fun.

This hard-to-find data was one major headache that the mothership project needed to overcome if it was going to have a chance of success. Databases flowed in with no explanation from Mikey. I imagined him drinking beer on hidden beaches, moving from one adventure to another across the region with women who had access to local business names. He was like the James Bond of Rotary Club lists.

Back in our office, getting business partners to work with us was not going well.

In retrospect, the reason was obvious. The cash the partners had expected with few strings attached was now going to us, and we would be running some Western-conceived marketing programs on their behalf. *Oh, by the way, we're going to need you to report back everything for documentation purposes. The reporting would be... thorough.* The mothership had also changed reporting requirements for partners, making them submit reems of new paperwork. Since we were the ones explaining these new rules, we were getting the blame. *So, when can we start?*

Imagine for a moment that you manage a company in the United States, and a Chinese national with a very strong accent calls up telling you that the annual funds are no longer coming. Instead, you have the option to participate in a heavily monitored campaign that traditionally has a low success rate. Also, you are going to work with this foreign agency you've never heard of and be required to complete a lot of new paperwork and reporting. Oh, yes, you are also expected to commit to your special piece of the Number. Failure to do so may result in a reduction of benefits to your partner status. Too bad if your sales target is higher than your annual total revenues. Also, you have to sell expensive products into smaller markets.

You might just tell the caller to buzz off or worse. Well that's what happened to us, but this is where the cultural communication piece kicked in.

The way most business partners told us *no* was by saying *yes*.

On these calls, we almost always got a *yes*. These *yesses* actually meant *no*. In fact, they were closer to "buzz off." We were working across indirect communicating cultures, which helped explain these responses.

Our team with Western accents was calling partners and explaining the new arrangement. The partners immediately reached out to their local contacts at the mothership to find out what is going on. Their contacts at the mothership either had yet to be briefed on this big change (which made the whole thing sound even more disorganized than it already was) or were aware of it and didn't like it.

In fact, they were right to be suspicious. To them, this was the United States headquarters inserting a Western agency to do things by the book. So, while we were in a situation that was already against us, we were using Western interns who made it even worse because it reinforced the idea that a bunch of foreigners were taking over.

The vision of globalized campaigns had now collided with local reality

This wasn't to say we didn't try to push back. There were a number of awkward global video calls with mothership executives across the world where we laid out the facts, but our words fell on deaf ears and blind eyes. One particularly confounding meeting ended with us showing pictures of one city's dirt roads and explaining the lack of any business large enough to want, or need, a $50,000 hybrid cloud system. The Mad Hatter was on her computer fiddling with a spreadsheet and declared, "This is our job. We do the impossible every day."

Indeed.

The mothership's process to set up each campaign took 38 PowerPoint slides to explain. With 120 partners with multiple campaigns each, this was a bureaucratic nightmare. And if the process was not followed correctly, we did not get paid.

We were told that a new global procurement system was launched designed to make invoicing easy. In this case, it was a unified worldwide billing system. Finally, a glimmer of hope that twenty-first-century global systems existed where standardization would make our lives easier.

Not so fast. This billing system was up and running, but even though the mothership's country offices said they were using it, they weren't—another case of saying yes but meaning something else. Instead, we had to get local approval and physically mail out the hundreds of invoices to each office.

To see how this giant company *really* operated worldwide was eye-opening. After all the talk and fancy slides and charts, one only had to scratch the surface to see this was a collection of small local tribes each doing things their own way. Local teams were unwilling to change, and senior managers were unwilling to find out what was really going on. Middle managers were left clinging to spreadsheets and transferred to new roles every 12 to 24 months before any real accountability landed on their desk. There were around 50 people from the mothership who worked on our project during the first year. By the end of year two, they were all transferred to new roles.

It was like the tea party scene from *Alice in Wonderland* where characters hop around the table speaking nonsense. The Mad Hatter was right, they were doing the impossible every day, chasing a white rabbit with no chance of catching it.

And then there was the small issue with currency. Initially, we were asked to price everything in US dollars (USD). Because the country offices were not using their own global billing system, it meant each country required programs be billed in local currency. In Vietnam, all the documents had to be changed from USD to dong. But headquarters fought back, so at their request we dropped the dong and went back to the dollar. Then we had to change the proposals in dong but track everything in dollars. Each change affected the precious 38-page setup process. The rule was that if the process wasn't done correctly, we didn't get paid. Dong. Dollar. Dong. Dollar. Back and forth it went.

This reality of the situation was growing clearer by the day, and the stress was beginning to show. I distanced myself from friends and family. My jaw ached constantly from gnashing my teeth. Working 17-hour days while trying to navigate ridiculous changes and procedures that often contradicted themselves caused me to go numb. Any sense of the larger business purpose vanished. It was now survival mode, but in a strange and self-punishing way. For reasons I've never understood, my phone was set to beep every time I got a new email, and I never turned it off. This project had "owners" across the globe, so the chatter was 24/7. *You said you could get this done.* My few hours of sleep were constantly interrupted by the beeping. Emails never came with good news. Each beep was another reminder I had overreached, overpromised, and underdelivered. This was all my fault. It was my mobile telltale heart.

Despite the complexities and my descent toward a mental and fiscal breakdown, partners slowly signed up. We were understaffed and had people in both the mothership and the partner community actively working against us, but things were moving. We needed more lists of prospects. Mikey J continued to deliver. Every few weeks a new batch of data came in. He was rumored to be in Vietnam and then disappeared in the Philippines where, somehow, he found a new jackpot of data.

"Don't ask" read the email subject line. There was no note, only a giant database attached.

How to win locally but fail globally

Our Indonesia work was going especially well. Campaigns went live, results came in (from larger cities, which made sense) and we were slowly showing a trend line that brought us closer and closer to the white rabbit. Why Indonesia? The woman running the team in Jakarta was a sweet, soft-spoken woman in her mid-40s. Her name was Yanti. She was inconsistent with her reports, didn't speak English well, often missed team meetings and didn't seem to have a full grasp of the overall program. So, what was she doing right?

One incident explained it: as I was chasing Yanti for a report, she texted saying she was in the hospital visiting one of the business partners who was recovering from complications of childbirth. She had been at this woman's bedside for the last two days. There was no father around, so Yanti decided to help.

I didn't know Yanti very well at the time, but she was the kind of person who prioritized helping people, even strangers, over her daily work responsibilities. How many people do that? I mean, *really* do that?

Yanti's secret was that she spent large amounts of time with people, and the actual work came second. In return, partners gave Yanti what she needed, which was results. I spent all my time poring over unrealistic spreadsheet assumptions and perplexing Power-Point slides. She was focused on the people regardless of deadlines. And what she did worked. Unfortunately, because we didn't get the paperwork sent in on time and the updates were often unclear, Yanti's relationship-building efforts were not acknowledged up the corporate food chain. We had happy partners and growing pipelines, but because she kept missing meetings with the mothership and not getting the corporate rituals right, the Mad Hatter wanted her removed.

We were starting to crack the code, at least in one country. But the Indonesia success was an example of a program that worked locally but failed globally. We had managed to get through all the obstacles and show a fighting chance of success, but process was more important than victory. Yanti wasn't filing reports correctly. Partners weren't filling in the paperwork the right way, either. The metrics looked different. Even though deals came in, they weren't coming the way the mothership wanted. After the first year of the project, I was told to replace Yanti. *Off with her head!*

Firing Yanti made it clear the entire project was doomed. Local differences varied too much to fit into a global standard, at least based on the parameters we were working within. Indonesia's success should have been the proof that we could get this done, but because this win was being rejected, it meant we would not be able to find a way out of this rabbit hole.

We limped through the first year, battered and bloodied. The delayed payments meant the program was running on a skeleton crew, leaving me working seven days a week, handling each of the many hundred proposals, invoices, reports, and countless review calls. One Sunday, I walked down to the local post office to buy stamps for the dozens of invoices that needed to be mailed out, only to find the office closed. Of course it was closed, it was a Sunday, but that was the kind of thing my brain had stopped thinking about many months earlier. I remember leaning on the locked door and breaking down into tears.

I was a mess. Each night, as I dealt with financing, I got chewed out on conference calls with those who managed the Number back in US.

Why was Malaysia going so slowly?

It's Ramadan.

Why did the Philippines completely stop for a week?

Because the Pope showed up and the city declared a five-day holiday and shut down the telecom systems.

What about Thailand?

There's another coup.

Vietnam?

A monsoon wiped out the power in Da Nang.

Where's Yanti?

Helping a business partner give birth.

It went on and on.

I had not paid myself for 12 months in a row and was starting to have days where I lay in bed unable to move for hours at a time. The phone beeped next to me. I struggled to do simple tasks. The act of replying to an email seemed overwhelming. My jaw ached.

We got through the first year and while woefully short of catching the white rabbit, we had managed to get enough of a flow going that we were making progress. Half of our contacts at the mothership had already been transferred, and new people came in, rightly so, asking what in the hell we were up to. Some decided they didn't like our people and forced them out. Typical company politics. Year two kicked off with a new, higher sales target. The rabbit was off and running again!

Even though the ongoing payment delays kept us virtually broke, the decision was made to invest in more people to attack year two with more force. Every penny that came in went out to keep up with payroll. Technically, we were making more than we were spending, but the outrageous payment terms strangled our ability to get much done. Still, we loaded the boat with new hires.

Then, out of nowhere, we got fired—without getting fired. The mothership once again changed the rules, this time by allowing partners the choice of how they wanted to spend their MDF. Where the money had gone directly to us, now business partners could do whatever they wanted with the money. The woman who took over had been one of the people quietly sabotaging the global approach from day one. We were finished.

I remember being in the Philippines training new hires when I heard the news. We had just massively increased our team. Now, all of these new hires had to be laid off. In the Philippines, this was expensive due to restrictive separation pay laws. I wrote the checks without much of a fight, oddly relieved the whole thing was collapsing.

Aside from the lawsuits and threats of lawsuits from landlords, employees, and subcontractors, taking apart our system was surprisingly quick. The ease with which our program could be disassembled was proof of how tenuous the whole thing was. The program didn't close down so much as evaporate.

The next year, word came back that all partners reported—wait for it—100% success. All targets were hit. The impossible had been achieved. Incredible.

More incredible was that a month after that, the entire program was shut down with no further information provided. Everyone at the mothership was moved to new roles. Rumors swirled of local managers faking their partner results, but these stories were quickly forgotten as the chase for the white rabbit continued.

The failure in hiding failure

By erasing the program so completely, nobody learned from the few successes and many mistakes. Our team in Indonesia did a great job, even though their achievement had been ignored because they weren't doing things the way headquarters wanted.

There was a lesson here. Global programs can work, but they require levels of flexibility and adaptability that many systems were unable to handle. Creative and adaptive behaviors, the skills so often touted across organizations, got punished rather than rewarded within systems obsessed with standardization. This needed to change. One thing about globalizing human-led projects was that the one-size-fits-all model needed to be broken apart and rebuilt, often from scratch.

Perhaps the biggest failure was the mothership's unwillingness to learn from the failure of the program. The entire effort collapsed, and the only thing that could make such a loss worthwhile was to learn from what had happened. It seemed no one was interested in this, which made the effort seem even more meaningless.

I spent the next two years chasing hundreds of unpaid invoices scattered across the region. Our plan to unify a global marketing program had shattered into tiny local pieces.

Survival Guide Tips:

- ✔ To build processes that work effectively in local situations, talk to the people on the ground. Spreadsheets only tell part of any business story.

- ✔ Break processes and systems that don't scale globally. Develop an appetite for creative destruction to break and rebuild. Human-focused global strategies are out there, they just have not been discovered yet.

- ✔ Don't hide from failure. Confront it and ask what can be learned for the future.

Chapter 10

The Ghost in
the Machine

"New beginnings are often disguised as painful endings."

—Lao Tzu

This chapter looks at specific ways to build a global team—and what happens when you do it in practice. Here are ways to make it happen. It takes patience, but it works.

WHILE MY mothership saga wound down, a geopolitical drama was heating up in Singapore. The booming local economy had driven up costs, including housing, food and transportation, causing some locals to feel they were being left behind. Under political pressure, the country decided to take protectionist actions, making it harder to bring in foreign talent—especially for entry-level jobs. *Singapore first* became the new rallying cry as the small city-state sought to balance local sentiment against outside global forces. Even though there weren't many locals interested in this kind of work, it became prohibitive to bring fresh graduates from overseas.

Yes, I had figured out how to find local talent, but I needed language skills to cover the entire region. Finding locals with bad grades and a good attitude was hard but manageable. Finding those who could also speak Vietnamese or Khmer was nearly impossible. Also, the foreigners were willing to work for free. My mama-san-inspired business model had worked out well but was poorly suited to handle the local business environment.

Restrictions on importing foreign workers hit everyone, and large companies with money started scooping up whatever talent they could find. The biggest technology companies—my clients—began poaching my people. Do-Not-Hire clauses were meaningless against giants with deep pockets, government connections and codes of conduct written and monitored from headquarters thousands of miles away. Smitty was right—the rule of power was more important than the rule of law. One large US client hired my last foreign employee, canceled our project without fully paying and had him build their own in-house team. In emerging markets, anything goes.

I had made a critical error. Because I could not find enough local talent, I had imported people from other parts of the world. While this solved short-term problems, it doomed any long-term potential of building a sustainable and locally relevant business. Moving to the other side of the world and filling an office with people who looked and thought like me was no way to win locally. Now I was paying the price.

Still burned out from the mothership experience, I closed the Singapore office and focused on a single location in Manila, as well as hired a handful of remote workers scattered across the region from the Middle East to Japan to cover local language needs. As I rebuilt, the number one thing I wanted to get right was to get everyone comfortable working on their own without a lot of guidance. Remote teams only work well when people feel comfortable speaking up when they need help. In other words, I wanted a flat organizational structure, but I now understood that in so many parts of the world, strong hierarchies die hard. To build this international team the right way, I reconnected with the one person with the track record for breaking this paradox, Mr. Axel. I wanted to know how he did it so well.

How to flatten hierarchies

Our reunion back at his condo pool began with a surprise. Axel had lost his job and was placed on what was politely referred to as "gardening leave."

"They shit-canned me, which, considering the situation, was the right thing to do," he said, cracking open a Tiger beer. It was 10:30 a.m. on a Tuesday.

So why did he lose his job? I turned down his offer for a drink as he told me what happened.

His was a German company that made industrial safety equipment, items like police armor, firefighting machinery and all sorts of hooks, fasteners and gadgets that helped people stay safe in dangerous situations. With more than a 100-year operating history, they made money, but their revenues were slowing and profits shrinking. The world was changing, but the company was not. Customers across the globe kept asking for, and expecting, different services.

Their requests varied. One part of the world wanted new products, another part wanted local post-sales support, another expected them to match local competition's service level guarantees. Everyone wanted lower prices as Chinese competition reaped destruction on their industry. Sure, the Chinese stuff was crap, but every year it got better.

Around 2013, the company spent gobs of money on one of the largest management consulting firms that gave them shiny and forward-sounding advice. Their consultants spoke with confidence. Their spreadsheets were beautiful. Their slick presentations outlined a plan: spread decision making out to local markets. Distribute power to the regional offices to allow more flexibility and let offices adapt to local needs. In other words, flatten the hierarchy. The company that had been operating across the globe for decades was now beginning the next phase to becoming global. It was a perfect situation for Axel and his leadership skills.

He had been running their Singapore office, the largest in the region. Everyone at headquarters liked Axel, because, even though he was Dutch, he somehow seemed to understand the Germans better than most, including some of the Germans. More important, he kept quiet and delivered results without causing much trouble, which, according to the Germans, was very un-Dutch. As the management consultant's plan was rolled out, Axel found he had more authority than before, including the ability to make decisions without going through headquarters' tedious approvals process. He was told to work closely with the other country heads across the region, in this case a team of 10 people. Axel was the only Westerner in the group.

"Many companies do this with or without an expensive management consulting firm telling them what to do. I knew exactly when and why this was going to get messed up, so I was already ahead of other regions."

He was referring to the challenge of flattening hierarchies in regions that were not used to this kind of change. He knew that taking power away from people in Germany who did not want to lose it and distributing it to people across Asia who did not know what to do with it was a difficult process. The real-world difficulties of this transformation were rarely included in shiny global expansion presentations.

TOR of Duty

Axel's plan was simple, subtle and flexible. "The Germans hated it," he says. "They kept trying to reengineer my regional leadership sessions by prioritizing revenue as the number one topic. For me, that was on the bottom of the list."

Axel had everyone meet at a resort in Thailand for two and a half days. Ten leaders, including Axel, from 10 different nationalities—all of whom suddenly had more authority to run their countries. But this new power also meant more responsibility. Headquarters made it clear that revenue targets would be watched carefully. This new power meant there were a lot more people watching them than ever before.

Things got chaotic, because while budgets and other pieces of corporate strategy had been handed down to the region, it was unclear how much authority was being distributed. There was also a sense that some back in Germany who saw power shifting away from their office were hoping it would fail. Some from headquarters passive-aggressively fought back by refusing to hand over documents, slowing down approvals, and in some cases disrupting client orders.

"We had to work together in ways never done before within the company. We realized we didn't know each other at all. They all thought I was German and were surprised when they found out I was an outsider too. That was when I said, 'OK guys, we need to friggen' slow things down before we move forward.'"

Axel built the off-site meeting's agenda. Revenue targets didn't come up once during the two and a half days. Instead, the teammates spent time digging into all the ways each of their countries worked differently and learning more about each other. His intention was to build trust before doing anything else.

They wrote down and discussed answers to questions such as *the biggest thing people don't understand about my country is…* and *the first piece of advice in order to succeed in my country is…* Everyone presented, debated, laughed and argued. They told stories about their families and shared pictures and videos. "It was great because we weren't talking about the company specifically, we were getting to know one another. We were building trust." Without a flow chart or PowerPoint, Axel was leveling the playing field. He was flattening the hierarchy.

Next Axel looked at similarities. The team discussed and debated values and working styles. *A time we worked well across regions was… Here's why it worked…* They found a lot of beliefs that overlapped, and they found some that did not. The objective of the exercise was to create their own personalized value system that everyone in the group was in sync with. In the end, they decided on three main values:

- Truth
- Openness
- Respect

Each of the three was defined. "This takes a while because all three can be defined in very different ways," explains Axel. "The more obvious the words, usually the more complicated they really are," he said. *Respect* for one person may mean withholding information to avoid making someone else uncomfortable. For another, showing respect may mean giving tough feedback, so this needed to be explored and worked out. How does respect relate to *openness*, for example? To many in the group, being *truthful* and *open* often came into conflict with being *respectful*. They discussed examples. They poked and prodded at cultural norms that had tripped up teams in other work situations. From there, they came up with agreements as to how they would work together through personality and cultural differences.

"It was a very personal and customized agreement. It's something everyone needs to work through. There's no easy formula here that asshole Americans like you constantly look for," he said with a smile, because he knew that was exactly what I was looking for.

With their new team communication contract, the group created goals for their own countries. "We thought of it like a pizza. Everyone built their own slice with all the stuff they wanted to accomplish, and then we put it all together. That led us to build milestones and ways to measure progress. We left that session feeling like a band of brothers. We had a great regional plan and called it our TOR of Duty." Trust. Openness. Respect. Three words that sounded simple, but they had to debate each one before everyone was clear on what they meant.

Everyone agreed on checkup calls. Not the monstrous 10-person conference calls, but one-on-one calls where everyone checked in on each other acting as peer-coaches. Axel called the Vietnam guy and chatted. The next week he'd have a call with the Indonesia head. They were all tasked with making sure the plans were progressing. Issues came up all the time, of course, but the team now felt as though they had nine other colleagues who had their back and would help.

Axel also had country heads present updates from *other* countries. This meant that leaders had to get to know details on another country's progress in order to deliver an intelligent update. During these information exchanges, gaps and issues were identified and the leaders from the different countries got enough information and experience to offer helpful advice. The country heads hated it at first because it took up a lot of time, but after only a few weeks, the effort started paying dividends. "We all knew exactly what the other countries were doing, and the group calls became much more focused. We came up with new ideas and tweaked existing ones. It was much better than normal team call bullshit," said Axel. "I was so proud of that group." Beneath Axel's rough language was a caring guy who knew how to get the best out of his team.

Axel saw the world differently than most. At first glance, it seemed as if he saw people as a network of relationships flowing, or, more often, broken due to behavioral differences and different approaches to power dynamics. He saw puzzles that wanted to be solved. But this was half right. Axel was misunderstood because he had focused so much energy on the differences within the team, in fact he was always driving at how to manage and minimize those differences. When he got his teams to overcome those differences, the results were fantastic. The journey he brought people through was filled with adversity and vulgarity, but the outcome was a battle-ready global team. That is why he was so good at what he did.

His results stood in stark contrast to the other regions of the company, which did not do as well. The new approach to allowing regions to take more autonomy got interpreted in very different ways. The Paris office was now in charge of managing Europe, Russia, Middle East, and Africa. These teams never met. Same with the Americas. In the Americas, the lead office, based in Arizona, was completely hands off. If each country in North and South America was responsible for their own territory, then it was up to each country to work through their own problems. There were no regional meetings. Arizona only wanted sales and revenue figures sent to them. Conference calls focused entirely on what was in the spreadsheets. Few spoke to Axel's American counterpart. He looked at the role of regional leader as symbolic. His United States market was the largest, and he really didn't care about the smaller Latin America groups. Since the US team was not getting compensated to help the other nearby regions, the Americans focused on their market and assumed everyone else was doing the same.

In France, they took the opposite approach to executing the new model. The French manager established a strict command-and-control-style reporting function across all 18 countries, from northern Europe to Russia to South Africa. No budgetary decisions could be taken without Paris's approval. One of the African leaders said, "The reporting shifted from Germany to France, only this time it was even worse than before. I had to get seven people in Europe to sign off if I was to take a flight to one of my own regional offices. Then there was separate documentation if I stayed at a hotel. A $40 dollar-a-night hotel! It was crazy. My hands were tied."

Axel's group outperformed all the other teams. After a tough start they grew while managing to keep costs down. "We had rebuilt a strong culture, which meant few people left. We saved a load of money that way."

Sadly, the safety device industry was stagnating across the globe. Cheaper competitors were flooding the market. "We were the best performers in an industry that wasn't performing," he said.

Headquarters didn't like what they were seeing, or more specifi- cally, didn't like the fact that they couldn't see what was going on in these newly empowered regions. Complaints from the Germans, who never wanted to lose control of things in the first place, com- bined with lackluster results gave the detractors enough reason to pull everything back to headquarters. The company hired another expensive management consulting firm that also used fancy graphs and presentations and advised the company to bring the power *back* to headquarters. After all, a centralized business could maintain greater control, reduce costs, and provide a more unified and consis- tent brand to the global marketplace. Three years after giving power to the regions, they reversed course and pulled everything back to Germany.

In Axel's region, partners and employees were confused by the reversal. One reseller canceled their contract, telling Axel privately that his company seemed too erratic to invest time and energy in. Employees across Asia who saw their influence diminish lost face in front of clients and colleagues. They became less engaged with their work. Many quit.

Mr. Axel, the man who took a disparate group of leaders and

turned them into a strong and integrated executive team that trusted each other, was asked to find work elsewhere. He was paid four months of gardening leave. I sat there by the pool amazed at how nonchalant he was about the whole thing. Wasn't he frustrated that all that effort had been wasted? "Not at all. This is the age we live in. That team of country heads I was a part of, they will all go somewhere and do great things. They will all make other people better."

Not long after, Axel took a role at a large petrochemical company in Mexico City. The last I heard he had started his team-building effort all over again.

Axel offered me some parting words: "You have made great progress. I have watched you go from a giant American asshole to a much smaller one. You have stopped rushing to conclusions. You consider situations from different angles. You know why your white rabbit project failed. Now, slow things down and focus on the people, not the process."

My profane Yoda was right. I had learned so much and I was ready to rebuild a team.

How old behavior can come back to haunt you

Reinvigorated, I left Axel and headed to Manila. First up, everyone on my team had to take a behavioral profiling test, and we all shared our results. We used the cross-cultural data that showed how our working styles differ. We had honest, sometimes difficult conversations about how we needed to handle conflict and how we had to push back if anything was unclear. We began to flatten the hierarchy in our own way.

Slowly, we made real progress and client satisfaction and retention become higher than ever before. The added focus on building the team's global mindset was paying off to the point where the team was handling things on their own, which freed up a lot of my time.

Until the mumu.

One day an employee saw a ghost in the hallway of our office. Called mumus (pronounced "moe moes"), these ghosts wander the Philippines and bring bad luck. A small group of employees asked that something be done to get rid of the mumu. The general manager, an Australian, didn't take the situation seriously. I was back in Singapore at the time and didn't take it seriously, either. Mumu jokes began circulating the office via emails. It seemed like the issue was not a big deal. But we were wrong. The small group that asked for something to be done grew larger. The next day, half the office did not show up for work. Polite requests to return turned to threats. Neither worked, as more and more of the team refused to come to the office. Clients began threatening to end their contracts with us because we weren't getting work done. This quickly cost us a small fortune.

After losing nearly a week's worth of work, I reconsidered the situation. We were trying to get the team to come back, but we were ignoring the real problem, which was the fake ghost. I instructed the general manager to find out how to get rid of a mumu. The answer was that we needed a priest to perform an exorcism. This cost us $20. He conducted a quick ritual involving chanting and holy water and five minutes later, it was over. Job done. "Send me the invoice," I sighed, wondering what my accountants would say.

The mumu really did haunt me. It was a painful reminder of how easy it was to let your guard down and forget how something so unimportant to one person can be deadly serious to someone else. We had made great progress in getting the team communicating the same way, and I was proud of our small but effective team. Yet everything could still be lost by a single mistake. I thought I had made it to that fourth and final level—the level where a person is able to adapt to any global situation without even thinking about it. I thought I had become *unconsciously competent*, but the mumu incident was a harsh reminder that I was still learning. I will always be learning.

There was one person who appreciated the mumu story.

Claire the Bulldog was about to move back home, and I wanted to reconnect before she left. Her husband's contract was up. His company was under pressure to reduce the number of expats, as they cost too much money. The sun was setting on the era of exorbitant expatriate packages, and companies were looking for locals to step up and take management roles traditionally held by visiting leaders from headquarters.

With Claire leaving, Texas Joe was done throwing money into the region. Rather than hire a replacement from the US, he switched to a full distributor model where a local company handled sales for the region. He sent out a news release positioning the partnership as an exciting APAC growth play, when in reality it was a retreat. This was a common smoke-and-mirrors play used by companies to maintain the illusion of growth. As a sign of stubbornness, his news release included images of baseball players.

We stood in Claire's half-full apartment as a group of movers packed their belongings for the long trip back to Texas. I told her about the ghost, and she laughed and told me I should have known better. We had both changed so much in the past few years. When Claire arrived in Asia, she would have lost her mind at the thought of having to hire a priest to banish a ghost. Now we both looked at it as just another day at the office.

Ironically, just as Claire was figuring things out, it was time for her to head home and focus on the domestic market.

Everyone makes expensive mistakes going global

Having spent the last few years stuck in the global bureaucratic stranglehold of the mothership, it was time to get back out in the world and start networking. Every time I got into a conversation about my experiences and the global leadership lessons I had learned, others had equally incredible stories to share.

We've been through three managing directors in three years.
We have no local leaders who are ready to run things, and we
*   don't know what to do about it.*
We pulled out of that country and lost $10 million.
Our offices in different countries don't communicate with
*   each other and clients are furious.*
The team we partnered with in that country was useless, so
*   we moved everything back home, wasting two years of*
*   development time.*

Everyone, it seems, was trying to work through these growing pains. Whether at an individual, team, or even companywide level, the headaches of working across regions were real and, for many, costly. Even companies operating worldwide for decades were having problems. One university whose focus was teaching next-generation global leadership asked for help improving their team communication across their international campuses.

I would go into a company with the objective of helping them with sales and marketing and leave with contracts helping their executive teams work together better around the globe. They wanted what was in the global survival kit. Workshops, seminars, and consulting engagements began taking up more of my time. This was a long way from the afterwork expat bar sessions where we'd toss stories around hoping people picked up lessons here and there.

When slap dragons go west

There was another trend happening. Businesses from emerging markets were expanding *west*. Unsurprisingly, they too were wrestling with the hidden cultural factors that came with overseas expansion.

Showing up in a foreign market and doing things the way they were used to back home doesn't work *anywhere* in the world. When coming into Western markets, the shock comes when strong hierarchies collide with flat hierarchies.

The people in the Welsh town of Cardiff in the UK experienced this firsthand.

Football (soccer for the United States) is a passion, and the Cardiff City Football Club has ardent fans. Around Cardiff, tattoos of bluebirds and the football club's blue crest cover forearms and biceps. Cardiff sports fans are faithful because, like the ink, team loyalty in this old mining town runs deep.

A few years ago, the club hit financial trouble, and Malaysian billionaire Vincent Tan stepped in with cash and conditions: he insisted the team color change from blue to red, and that the Welsh dragon become the main emblem, replacing the bluebird.

Why did he want the beloved bluebird awkwardly demoted to the bottom of the new, red logo?

This was part of his international growth plan. The idea was to expand the team's fan base into Asia. In theory, the dragon—a symbol of Wales and already on the Welsh flag, and also popular in many Asian cultures—would be welcomed by both Welsh supporters and the larger Asian audience Tan sought to cultivate.

The change was supposed to be a fusion of Eastern and Western cultures. Tan's vision made sense in theory, but good luck selling that to the local bluebird die-hards. While new fans in Malaysia may have liked the modifications, Cardiff supporters were furious.

Even followers of Cardiff's archrival Swansea City thought the change was intolerable. The chant "We'll always be blue" began reverberating across Cardiff City Stadium at the 19:27 mark of each match—a reference not only to Tan's changes but also to the year 1927, the last time the team won the FA Cup. Ignoring the uproar, Tan pushed ahead with his plan while local fans stood by, unable to comprehend how someone could come in and make such an audacious change.

After three years of conflict, the traditional blue logo made its triumphant return to Cardiff, albeit with an out-of-place little red dragon snarling at the base. As of 2019, Tan's management approach seems to have changed. He had grown into the role and won back the support of many of the fans. This was one of a growing number of Eastern organizations struggling to adapt to Western ways of "how things are done around here."

As outside investment continues to grow into markets in the west, these differences in leadership styles quickly become more of a challenge. I coached one Indian client who was trying to figure out how to work with Americans. He did not understand the feedback they were giving him and why they were not responding to his detailed email requests. Using data, behavioral profiling, and good old-fashioned experience, together we changed his entire approach, which included getting to the point faster, asking clarifying questions and, yes, checking up on how the Chicago Bulls were doing in the playoffs.

Clients from Singapore, Philippines, the Middle East, India, and elsewhere echoed the same point: working with Americans can be confusing. Coaching sessions focused on understanding how Americans tend to provide feedback (saying something nice, giving the actual feedback, and then saying something nice again) as well as their norms for group conversations and when it is a good idea to speak up. Like everyone, adjusting to styles different from our own required a level of flexibility and stepping outside of comfort zones.

Changing with the times

The Singapore government changed employment rules, exposing a critical weakness in my business model. It forced me to evolve and rebuild a remote team across the region. I used Axel's advice and focused on understanding the power distance I was up against. Using the survival kit I had put together—behavioral profiling, cross-cultural data to define working similarities and differences between the team and all the other communication tools—I was able to build a battle-ready remote international group. It worked so well that it gave me free time to work with other organizations who wrestle with the same issues—not only Western companies, but organizations from all over the world that were growing into new markets.

Once again, my business evolved...accidentally.

Survival Guide Tips:

✔ First, build relationships. Second, get to work.

✔ Invest time for teams to build their own Communication Contracts. They should acknowledge working style differences and lay out a plan for overcoming them.

Chapter 11

Putting Together
the Global Pieces

"In the long history of humankind (and animal kind, too), those
who learned to collaborate and improvise most effectively
have prevailed."

—*Charles Darwin*

Organizations are global, people are not, but there is hope.
Concluding ideas on how to succeed across a shrinking planet.

IT'S RAINING HERE in Singapore. It is one of those storms that seems as if the end of the world is nigh; the heavens open and umbrellas are useless, until it suddenly passes, leaving a spectacular rainbow. Although my suit is getting soaked, my spirits can't be dampened because I am heading to a happy client. We're celebrating a big win. Actually, a big save, the salvaging of a relationship that was about to go south.

The client is a construction company headquartered in Germany, with a specialty in designing and installing soundproofing technologies for offices. They found themselves about to lose a large Indonesian customer based out of Jakarta. It was a simple cross-cultural gaffe, but one that nearly lost them a multimillion-dollar account. I was asked to help untangle the mess.

This screwup, like so many others, happened by accident. The Germans had invited an Indonesian CEO to a fancy event for their customers in Hamburg. The CEO said yes, adding that he wanted to bring his wife and some of his top executives with him because it would help build relationships between the two companies. Unfortunately, the invite was only for the CEO. No spouses. No executive team. With strong anti-corruption rules in the EU, no one would approve of including significant others to such an event. What was totally normal in Indonesia verged on corruption in Germany.

To the Germans, these strict rules were obvious, so informing the client did not seem like a delicate, deal-breaking matter. Without consulting anyone, an executive in Hamburg who worked on the account took the initiative to reply to the Indonesian CEO's request. To put it mildly, he was, well, German about it. Essentially, he said, "No, you can't bring your wife or other executive team members." As I had discovered years earlier, the word *no* can mean a lot of different things around the world. In a place like Indonesia, it is rarely used directly because it can come across as an insult, which is exactly how it was interpreted here. The German company had now upset their client, who was threatening to take his business elsewhere, making this a potentially expensive mistake.

I showed the team members in charge of the Indonesia account the datasets used by Jake the Snake, specifically how communication styles differ between Germany and Indonesia. The two countries were on opposite sides of this spectrum with Germany being extremely direct and Indonesia extremely indirect. I gave examples. Some of the company's executives in Germany had no idea that a straightforward no could be so damaging. How could they? Unless they spent a lot of time wandering around the Indonesian archipelago, it's unlikely that the guy who fired off what he thought was a simple email knew all these things. That's why the cross-cultural data was so helpful to new business nomads. This was the cheat sheet that visualized the differences. It was up to us to figure out what to do about it.

While the issue started out as an email misunderstanding, simply changing communication styles was not going to fix the underlying problem. What was happening in this case were two different views of how business *relationships* should be built. The Germans wanted an organized customer event, but the Indonesian CEO thought differently. He was used to business events that included more of his team as well as family members.

It dawned on the German team that if they were going to keep this valuable account and find others like it, they needed to adapt how they built relationships. But first they needed to save the account, so we looked at more cross-cultural data sets focusing on relationships. In some parts of the world, business relationships were more task-based, like in Germany. If both sides got a task completed as agreed, this usually built trust quickly. *She got the job done, which means she is reliable; therefore, I like her and will work with her again.* In Indonesia, relationships tend toward the personal. *Before I work with this person, I need to get to know her first.* This may require more meals, more time spent on non-work-related topics or, like Yanti, my Indonesian account manager, more hospital visits. The irony was that the German company's attempt to build relationships by hosting a customer event had the opposite effect with this Indonesian client.

Saving a million-dollar client

It was a lot to untangle, but we worked through it and came up with a plan to fix things. I was using what I had learned from Axel, Jake, and the countless others I had encountered along the way. The plan had three parts.

One: *Treat people the way they want to be treated.* We got some of the key executives from Hamburg and Singapore to visit the CEO of the client company in Jakarta and start rebuilding the relationship. This wasn't a one-day trip. It required spending three days with the client, which is a lifetime to many of the task-based executives from Germany.

Two: *Treat interactions like a performance piece.* During the long haul to Indonesia, the executives needed to reimagine their communication approach. They worked on dialing down their directness and instead started using softening statements, like the messaging Jake gave his callers. Instead of, "no, we can't do this," they worked on phrases like, "I wonder if we could look at a few options to find something that works for everyone."

I used one recommendation from Professor Andy Molinsky[1] of Brandeis University: his advice is to treat international work encounters like a performance piece. In other words, become an actor. The German executives wrote out phrases and rehearsed their lines over many cocktails throughout their long flight.

Three: *Get rid of the box.* We brainstormed ideas to help reassure the Indonesian client he was a valued customer. The event organizers in Hamburg were not going to change their rules regarding invitations, so what to do? There were more Asian clients signing on each year, so this issue was not going to go away. The team I was working with felt boxed in by existing rules and processes. We did not want to think outside of the box, we wanted to get rid of it. It was decided that because there were so many new clients now throughout Asia, they could host a customer event specifically for clients across the region. They asked the Indonesian CEO to be their first keynote speaker.

The team was now thinking with a global mindset. A few months after the trip to Jakarta, word came back that the account was back on track and the first Asia customer appreciation event was in the works. That's why I was fighting for a taxi in the rain: we were celebrating saving this large account from a cross-cultural accident.

In the rain, taxi demand spikes, and one of the most transport-friendly cities in the world turns into a commuting nightmare. When the ride-sharing revolution hit Singapore, it was a godsend. Thank you for upending the old order of catching a cab, Uber.

However, I won't be typing my location into the Uber app today. It no longer works here. It no longer works in Cambodia, Indonesia, Malaysia, Myanmar, the Philippines, Thailand, and Vietnam because Uber lost out to a Singapore-based ride-hailing app called Grab. Even Uber, hailed as a worldwide growth success story, got tangled up in the complications of global business. Why did they lose? Once again, it came down to relationships and the company's inability to adapt to different ways of doing business. Uber tried to do their own thing their own way and came up against the realities of a big, complex planet.

Uber entered all these markets spending hundreds of millions of dollars, but local competitors managed to fight them off.

In a company blog, Dara Khosrowshahi, CEO of Uber, wrote, "One of the potential dangers of our global strategy is that we take on too many battles across too many fronts and with too many competitors."[2]

Some of these battles across Southeast Asia involved local competitors who were thinking about the ride-sharing business in profoundly different ways. Specifically, they were including a lot of additional local offerings, which set them apart from Uber's initial service. Package delivery, massage services, cosmetics, online games, auto repair, and house cleaning were all available through local ride-sharing apps, and these services varied considerably from market to market. I imagined Chen from Taiwan saying, "You see, everything is interconnected. It's all about the *relationships*, how things work together. You can't just go it alone, that is booshit!" Confucius would concur.

Not only did local ride-share companies create relevant services, those who took the lead were the ones that added an integrated payment option. Easier and cheaper than credit cards, the payment option enabled consumers to pay for any of the services within the apps' ecosystem as well as send and receive money to other people. These apps became a one-stop-shop for consumers, which was way bigger than ride sharing. Did the relationship-focused nature of the Eastern cultures play a role in the development of these interconnected technology platforms?

Uber also expanded into food delivery and other services, but local competitors in other markets were doing this from day one, and the services varied country-by-country, which left Uber struggling to keep up.

Uber was offering an individual service in parts of the world that were looking for collective solutions. They got tied up with the growth while forgetting to get tied in with local norms.

While Uber did get a stake in Grab's business as part of the agreement to leave the region, the fact that Uber apps here can no longer be used tells the story of who won that battle. Uber also left China, ceding the business to a local competitor called DiDi. Same with Russia when a company called Yandex took over.

Yes, local companies beat Uber in a number of markets. But how will these victors expand overseas? Here, it once again gets interesting. DiDi's expansion plans so far have taken a different route. With a major push into Latin America, Japan, Europe, and South Korea, their strategy has been to partner with local providers already established in those markets. The downside for DiDi is less control and potentially less of a unified brand presence, but the local market knowledge should help overcome some of the roadblocks that caused Uber's international breakdown.

In my experiences trying to manage a large partner program, it was clear that partnerships do not always work out as planned. Expect DiDi's ride into new markets to be bumpy.

Finally, a car sloshes through the puddles, tires spraying water, and picks me up. I chat with the driver about how he thinks the ride-share battles are going. The people like him on the frontline always have good insights. He says the competing ride-share firms keep trying to poach drivers from each other. The drivers love it because it means more money in their pockets, at least in the short-term. This doesn't sound like a sustainable growth plan though.

We stop talking as the radio DJ starts reading the news headlines: international treaties being revoked, populist politicians gaining power, protectionism on the rise, threats of trade wars. It goes on and on. What a disruptive world. We seem to be heading into an era of continued fragmentation rather than one of unification. And yet, within these fragments, global business opportunities abound.

Frustrated with the grim updates, the driver switches the English news to a Chinese station I cannot understand, but I'm feeling optimistic about where we are heading.

Global Mindset

I wrote earlier about behavioral profiling as a tool to improve how people understand themselves and those they work with. I've also introduced some of the cross-cultural research that looks at different working styles around the planet. Ultimately, the goal is for people to build what has been called a "global mindset." A friend of mine, Csaba Toth, started a company called ICQ Global and developed a tool called Global DISC, combining it with cross-cultural data. Here's how he defines a global mindset:

> Global mindset is the ability to see a situation from multiple per-
> spectives and flex our behavior so we can be competent and
> confident in most situations. It is knowing how to apply the blue-
> print of why people think and behave differently and the skills to
> turn those differences into synergy instead of painful liability.

Maybe the world isn't ready to speak as one unified voice. So be it. It
is our job to figure out how to navigate through it all. Because within
the different ways of seeing the world are different ways of solving
problems. The answers, like the problems we face, are found in various global pieces. The open-minded, curious, and adaptable people
thrive in such an environment.

From accidental to intentional

Global opportunities will continue to emerge from across all four
corners of this planet, but they will require local approaches to make
them work. This means that the tribe of accidental business nomads
will continue to grow. If you find yourself in this tribe, your goal
should be to grow from *accidental* to *intentional* by building up a
global mindset and looking for ways to adapt and evolve along with
this shrinking planet. It's not easy, but it's important to stop every
once in a while and enjoy the ride!

The rain is tapering off and, after 30 minutes of staring at a sea of
red lights and listening to mandarin talk radio, I make it to the meeting spot, a funky bar that takes full advantage of the lush tropical
vegetation surroundings. My glasses fog over immediately, air condi-
tioning fighting humidity. The awning is still dripping rain into the
potted exotic plants, but that doesn't stop crowds from huddling outside to puff their cigarettes. Inside, the team is already by the bar and
firmly in position, laughing and clinking glasses. There's a German,
an Indonesian, an Indian-Singaporean, and now me. It sounds like a
setup for a corny joke, but it's not, it's the new normal—a bunch of

different people all trying to figure things out. I place an order with the bartender and join the celebration.

"It's one-for-one," says the bartender.

Perfect.

Coda

The people I have written about in this book have all wrestled in their own ways with this journey toward developing their own global mindset. It is paradoxical that more people than ever are working globally but feeling isolated like they are alone in wrestling with these problems. What is so frustrating is that the efforts of so many people who have learned these lessons the hard way are lost on others. Their mistakes are covered up or ignored because a company's and an individual's priority is to protect brand, both corporate and personal. Hiding the truth prevents others from learning from past mistakes. This is why I wrote this book.

I want to tell these stories and to suggest a few shortcuts to all the accidental business nomads out there. You are not alone, and there are ways to make things work. From my own experiences and from the companies I have worked with, I have narrowed my focus to five skills that are needed to survive across a shrinking planet. They are:

- Communication
- Adaptation
- Confrontation
- Persuasion
- Creativity

Examples can be found throughout this book. Chen, my Taiwanese friend, would be quick to point out that all these skills are interconnected, and he would be right. It is also worth spending time thinking about each separately and then looking at how they work together. We can take the East and West approach and develop skills to help people work in any sort of global environment.

Communication. Jake the Snake spent his career trying to figure out how to sell products to complete strangers over the phone. He started with his native United States market until globalizing trends led him around the world, where he found that communication styles varied considerably. The American communication style he was used to didn't work overseas, so he searched for answers that came in the form of cross-cultural data sets from sources such as Geert Hofstede and the GLOBE Project. These studies attempt to define and measure communication styles around the planet. Sometimes they contradict each other, which is good. Humans are confusing, and more research like this needs to be done.

What the studies do agree on is that one of the most common problems that arises in global work situations occurs when direct communicators and indirect communicators misunderstand one another. The word *yes* can mean no and anything in between. Another Indian client of mine is working on how she speaks more directly with her Australian counterpart. She is realizing some of her responses can come across as vague. She is working on this. On the other hand, my client from Hamburg learned that no can be interpreted in many ways. That word resulted in an unplanned trip to Jakarta. Time consuming? Yes, but it saved a seven-figure account.

Adaptation. Some find the German/Indonesian example frustrating. I often hear pushback, especially by direct communicators, who think that indirect communicators need to be less sensitive and become more direct. While that may be one approach, cultural norms die hard. Sticking to one's opinions can be expensive. The question I ask is *Do you want to do things your way, or do you want to get results?* Working globally means you may get to choose only one. This is why adaptation is so important.

Mr. Axel, the crusty, serial expat, taught me to *treat people the way they want to be treated.* He was able to adapt naturally, or he at least made it look natural. He had been working around the world for decades, so he had a lot of time to practice. No matter what part of the world you are from, it is up to *you* to adapt. For most accidental business nomads, adapting working styles is harder than it sounds. So, at first, consider acting the part. It is a novel way to get into the right mindset before and during a meeting or conference call.

Of course, a person cannot adapt until they first know the start and end points. "Who are you?" Axel asked. Many people don't know if they are direct or indirect communicators. They have never thought about it. I spent a lot of time in parts of the world where indirect communication is the norm, yet most people do not consider themselves indirect. It is like asking the fish, "How is the water?" The response is usually, "What is water?"

Behavioral profiling is a great way to start learning about yourself and those around you. It will teach you how to communicate and also how you behave in specific situations. DISC is one of the more popular frameworks, but there are several options to choose from. Research on personality types continues to evolve and this, along with advances in cross-cultural data collection, is another area worth watching.

Remember Axel's lunch secret? His secret wasn't having two lunches while visiting specific offices, but in understanding that relationships are built differently across the world. Some bond over lunch, some over drinks, some don't want to bond at all and simply focus on work. He knew how to read a situation and adapt.

Confrontation. Claire the Bulldog's working style was direct. She arrived overseas like so many senior managers: she was on a mission to plant a flag in foreign soil and start winning. She often got right to the point and focused on solving problems fast. This approach, a winning formula back home, did not work out the way she had planned.

Claire was naturally confrontational. She expected others to be the same. She hired Lionel, who naturally avoided confrontation. When she got loud, he went quiet, making the tension between the two worse. I have focused on Claire, but for the millions of Lionels out there, the lesson is equally valuable: it is necessary to adjust to the person you are trying to work with. This may sound frustrating to someone who likes to avoid confrontation, but we are all in this global situation together, and *everyone* needs to make changes.

Persuasion. Claire also needed to know how to better manage her boss back home. Texas Joe was not a one-off phenomenon. Over the years of my telling his *slap dragon* story, people felt comfortable sharing with me their corporate overseas challenges, especially trying to get HQ to adapt to local market conditions. How to persuade others when business environments are so complex and fast-paced?

The Centurions had many faults, but some of those guys knew how to manage diverse teams and how to manage their bosses, who were often based on other continents. Roger Staddon was good at giving his overseas managers data-driven examples through stories. I've come to think of this as a kind of *calibrated storytelling.* In a work environment, he was persuasive. He also listened closely to his local teammates and protected and defended them from the inconsistent guidance coming from their overseas headquarters. He seemed to decompress from this role by golfing naked.

Persuasion, like so many other working styles, varies across the planet. Professor Erin Meyer from INSEAD continues to publish research in this area.[3]

I was able to use her findings to help a French client recently. The French company was having trouble persuading their American client to use a new, more complex, financial reporting system. The French woman had been sending long, detailed, step-by-step instructions about how to use the system. The American seemed to be ignoring the notes. Meyer's research suggests that Americans tend to prefer messages that begin with a summary and then provide details later. French tend to go the opposite way, preferring to understand all of the principle data points first and getting to the conclusion, or summary, at the end.

This became an aha moment for my French client in her quest to understand why she had failed to persuade her American counterpart. She adjusted her next email by putting the summary first and *then* going into further detail. The next day her American counterpart responded for the first time saying he understood the request and followed her instructions.

Creativity. Creativity within a business setting happens when there is trust within a team. Trust to speak up, ask questions, disagree, and even to fail. Trust to try something you may not agree with. My hiring model, while borrowed from the mama-san at the bar, was a creative solution to a tricky problem. It was an example of acknowledging local market challenges and coming up with, what I thought at the time, was a good answer. In the short-term this plan worked well. The problem was that I had fallen into the same trap so many other Western companies were guilty of—I had filled my office with Westerners because I found them easier to work with. Many companies do this and end up with groups of people who all think and behave the same way.

Locals know local markets. So, hire locals. It is not always easy because of the different working styles discussed throughout this book. However, teams who invest time and resources on these five areas—Communication, Adaptation, Confrontation, Persuasion, Creativity—work better.

Confidence increases, people speak up more, and they feel comfortable sharing ideas—and this is the goal teams should aim for. This is how trust gets built. And, with a little intelligent leadership design, this is when cultural differences evolve from a liability to an asset.

I remember a conversation with Axel, late at night at yet another dive bar. Life, wild and exotic, paraded past on the street, with vendors selling laser pens and other colorful trinkets. Local children, whose stories were too awful to contemplate, sold roses and god knows what else. We talked and watched the procession of humanity from our street-facing barstools. Axel was in an especially philosophical mood. "We can talk about peoples' differences all day long. Of course, that is important, but we must get beyond those differences. We must achieve real trust if we want to make this global team stuff work. We have to actually care about each other." He went quiet for a bit and then he said something that summed up why he was so good at working globally. Saying to no one in particular, or to everyone, "All I ever wanted was for my team to know that I care."

Survival Guide Tips:

✔ Grow from an *accidental* to *intentional* business nomad by promoting global mindsets across your organization.

Conclusion

The Global
Survival Kit

"Don't drink at the hotel. Find out where the people who work
at your hotel do their drinking."

—Anthony Bourdain

THESE DAYS I continue to travel around the world, working with organizations that wrestle with global leadership challenges. Every company challenge is different, but the underlying obstacles of communication remain the same. Leaders today and in the future need to build global mindsets in order to break the habit of following old scripts. They need to build teams that have the trust to bring their best ideas forward. Often, I help people and teams get to the next level of this journey.

Over the years I have put together a few tools to help business nomads as they go global. I call it The Global Survival Kit. To wrap up this book, I'd like to present some of the key ideas and tools I recommend packing into your Global Survival Kit. Many of the origins of these tools came from the people I've met and situations I've been through. And hopefully it won't surprise you that it is constantly changing and adapting.

1. **Know yourself.** Research continues to come out showing strong leaders have higher-than-average levels of self-awareness.

   No one is perfect, so the need to understand strengths and weaknesses makes for an important first step in improving how you work with people across the globe. Hierarchies and various cultures around the globe make this one especially tricky. How do you show vulnerability in a part of the world where that is looked down on? How do you admit when you are wrong within an environment that punishes weakness? You have to first know yourself. Behavioral psychology assessments can be a good place to start.

2. **Cross-cultural data.** These issues are not new. Five hundred years ago, Magellan and his shipmates landed on islands across the south pacific, and local tribes would come on board ships and start taking trinkets and anything that wasn't bolted down. They were coming from a collectivist culture where the concept

of individual ownership did not exist. Their actions were interpreted by the significantly more individualistic Europeans as stealing. Situations escalated quickly, from yelling to pushing to weapons being drawn. People died, including Magellan, who never made it past the Philippines.

I'd argue that half a millennium later, we have not really progressed that much. Today cultures cross paths daily, with the purpose of building business ties and doing deals. While most interactions tend to work out well, work situations, as we have seen, can quickly spin out of control. From start-ups to world leaders, these issues can cost money and sometimes lives.

There is hope! There is data. Differences across cultures have been defined and continue to get measured. If you can measure it, you can manage it. At least that's the idea. While these datasets are far from perfect, they can be a great resource to better understand different working styles and how to adjust to interactions around the world.

3. **Learn to adjust in a moment of panic.** From being unable to order a cup of hot water to negotiating multimillion-dollar global contracts, we all get those *screaming on the inside* moments. If you know one of these moments is happening, PAUSE.

> *Pause.* Are you *screaming on the inside*? You aren't alone. Take a breath. When working through foreign situations, often gut responses can be wrong. So, before anything is said, pause.

> *Active Listening.* This may be the single easiest and yet most important tool to manage people, excel in sales, find a mate, handle networking events, negotiate, etc. And it is absolutely critical when communicating across cultures.

> *Use cross-cultural data.* With big-data flooding in from internet use around the world, expect a lot more research from this field in the coming years. The datasets we use today will look

archaic within the decade, but for the time being, they can be of great help to better understand cross-cultural differences.

See things from the other person's perspective. This is easy to say but hard to do. There are ways we can practice and improve how to see situations from different angles.

Elaborate. Possibly the easiest but least used approach for any conversation. Before allowing a conversation to end, double check the next steps or the key point made. Simple wrap-up statements include: "Before we end, can we quickly summarize the key points and next steps?" or "Can you feed back to me what you heard?" or "What is the specific next step here, and when will we reconnect to look at progress?"

4. **Communication Contracts.** Often the simplest words can be the hardest, *yes, no, trust, respect, openness,* etc. Invest time with teammates to lay out your communication rules. Establish guidelines to reduce misunderstandings.

    A strong communications contract should be a part of any global or regional team, both temporary or long term. Ideally this agreement should be created together as a team so everyone understands the purpose and everyone has a say. You may be surprised at where the conversations lead. This is a good thing. Get the surprises out early and get the fundamentals out in the open early.

5. **Share stories with friends.** In a majority of workshops I run, the first activity is to hear from the participants about cross-cultural challenges they have faced. The rooms start out quiet. So, I share one of the many stories I've picked up or been a part of. It could be a small moment trying to get directions or something much larger.

    A funny thing happens. Another person speaks up with a story. Then another, and another. Frequently, these issues, these frustrations have never been shared. Maybe people are concerned about sounding insensitive or maybe they are embarrassed and don't want to sound silly. But you can feel the energy in the room rise along with a sense of relief. Finding others who wrestle with these common international issues feels good. It builds connections and, often, friendships. We discover that most of us mean well even though we are frequently misunderstood.

We want to figure this stuff out. We want to understand differences, and we want to be understood by those we work with. But often organizations hide these culture clashes or ignore them. The stories get buried, erased or forgotten. We don't learn from our past mistakes. We miss opportunities to make new connections. This has perhaps been the most surprising finding from my work. The hesitation or, in many cases, deliberate actions to erase the past. I would love to say that companies have become better at going global since I started my own journey back in the first years of the twenty-first century. I have not seen much evidence for this. Sharing stories and building connections are one of the most powerful tools out there. So, tell your stories and learn from others! Good luck and enjoy the trip!

Endnotes

Chapter 2

1. Even if a product or service is banned in Singapore, it can still be a good place to set up shop. Airbnb and several companies selling vaping products, both illegal in Singapore, run their regional headquarters from the country.
2. Ivan Tan. "Outlook 2017: ASEAN Still Beckons." February 23, 2017, p. 10. https://ie.enterprisesg.gov.sg/-/media/files/asean-outlook-2017/presentation -materials/outlook-2017---asean-still-beckons.pdf?la=en.
3. Godfred Koi-Akrofi, "Mergers and Acquisition Failure Rates and Perspectives on Why They Fail," *International Journal of Innovation and Applied Studies*, 17(1), (July 2016): 150–158. https://www.researchgate.net/publication /305406845_Mergers_and_Acquisitions_failure_rates_and_perspectives_on _why_they_fail.

Chapter 3

1. Data from the 2004 Globe Study can be found here: https://globeproject.com /study_2004_2007?page_id=data#data An updated study is being released in 2020.
2. Data from Hofstede's work can be found here: https://www.hofstede-insights .com.
3. There are countless stories of British managers making similar statements and accidentally causing confusion among their teams. One woman I met told me her team's communication was "not too bad," and she meant it was bad enough they needed to invest in outside help to get it fixed.

Chapter 4

1. The Netherlands scores on most cross cultural data sets as being one of the most direct communicating countries in the world.
2. It is inadvisable (and illegal) to bribe border guards, so please do not do this.

Chapter 5

1. Peter Drucker is often given credit for this quote but there seems to be no evidence he ever said it.
2. Csaba Toth runs a company that does intercultural DISC assessments and training, combining cross-cultural data with the DISC model. I have used his tests in the past, but am not financially connected with the company. https://icq .global/.

Chapter 6

1. Neerja Jetley, "Singapore's Multimillionaires: New Wealth Report Busts the Myths," Forbes, September 27, 2013. https://www.forbes.com/sites/neerjajetley /2013/09/27/anatomy-of-a-singapore-multi-millionaire-a-new-wealth-report -busts-many-myths/#3a673713b76e.
2. Diksha Gera and Sharnie Wong, "These Asian Countries May Become the World's Largest Offshore Wealth Hubs," *Bloomberg Intelligence*, October 3, 2018. https://www.bloomberg.com/professional/blog/asian-countries-may-become -worlds-largest-offshore-wealth-hubs/.
3. Sean Coughlan, "Pisa Tests: Singapore Top in Global Education Rankings," BBC, December 6, 2016. https://www.bbc.com/news/education-38212070.

Chapter 7

1. Don't peel visa stickers out of passports; it is illegal and can invalidate the document.
2. Do people think differently in different parts of the world? This is a controversial question and much research has been done. *The Geography of Thought: How Asians and Westerners Think Differently…and Why* by Richard Nisbett is a good place to start.
3. "Greek Mathematics—Pythagoras," *The Story of Mathematics*, http://www .storyofmathematics.com/greek_pythagoras.html.
4. For more detail on these different working styles, especially around contracts, read Richard Conrad's book *Culture Hacks: Deciphering Differences in American, Chinese, and Japanese Thinking.*

Chapter 8

1. A few years after he worked for my company, Mikey sent me a chilling one-line text saying his mother's body had been found in a mini-mart bathroom. She had died from a heroin overdose.
2. Plague enthusiasts generally agree that the next major contagion will likely originate somewhere out of Southeast Asia. There are a number of reasons for this, including population densities, wildlife, climate, deforestation and the pesky habit of Chinese eating nearly every type of animal under the sun.
3. Frangoul, Anmar. "Counting the Costs of a Global Epidemic." CNBC, February 5, 2014. https://www.cnbc.com/2014/02/05/counting-the-costs-of-a-global-epidemic.html.
4. A few weeks later, Mikey contracted swine flu. He spent a few days in bed in his landlady's apartment.

Chapter 11

1. Andy Molinsky, "Global Dexterity: How to Adapt Your Behavior Across Cultures without Losing Yourself in the Process," *Harvard Business Review Press*, February 19, 2013.
2. Dara Khosrowshahi, "A New Future for Uber and Grab in Southeast Asia," Uber Newsroom, March 25, 2018. https://www.uber.com/newsroom/uber-grab/.
3. Erin Meyer, "The Art of Persuasion in a Multicultural World," June 15, 2014. https://www.erinmeyer.com/the-art-of-persuasion-in-a-multi-cultural-world/.

Do you want more
survival guide skills?

Go to www.leadershipnomad.com/businessnomad for additional bonus material including lessons, planning templates and articles and videos.